The Tradition of the
HIMALAYAN
MASTERS

The Tradition of the
HIMALAYAN
MASTERS

Pandit Rajmani Tigunait, Ph.D.

The Himalayan International Institute
of Yoga Science and Philosophy
of the U.S.A.
Honesdale, Pennsylvania

© 1993 by the Himalayan International Institute
of Yoga Science and Philosophy of the U.S.A.
RR 1, Box 400
Honesdale, PA 18431

03 02 01 00 99 98 97 96 95 94   8 7 6 5 4 3 2

ISBN 0-89389-134-7

Front cover photograph: The Himalayas at Kedarnath in
Uttarpradesh, India. A shrine at this famous pilgrimage site honors
Shankaracharya.

Dedicated to His Holiness
Jagadguru Rajagurutilaka
The Late Dr. Sri Shivarathri Rajendra
Mahaswamigalu

Contents

Sri Swami Rama of the Himalayas

Introduction
by Swami Rama

The tradition of the Himalayan sages is an unbroken chain extending for thousands of years, a living tradition that still exists today, undisturbed by the passage of time or other external changes. This tradition is not concerned with teachings that are limited in their applicability to any era of history or to any geographical region of the world— its entire emphasis is on the experience of that Truth which is eternal and universal. The realization of Truth is the highest goal of all existence, although at different times and places, a variety of terms have been used to describe this path.

The history of this ancient tradition remains shrouded in mystery. It is helpful for the modern student of meditation to understand this tradition and the lineage of sages who have carried on these teachings. But in seeking to study it, the student, no matter how sincere, is at a disadvantage: many of the ancient texts do not exist in translation, or even when they do, their teachings require clarification and interpretation if they are to provide seekers with any practical guidance.

The lineage of sages in the Himalayan tradition passed on their teachings in primarily oral fashion, with each sage transmitting this knowledge directly to prepared students. As Pandit Rajmani Tigunait explains, the unbroken chain of lineage goes back at least five thousand years, although Shankaracharya, the great philosopher and yogi, formally established the tradition 1,200 years ago.

The Vedas are the ancient texts and scriptures that contain the wisdom of these ancient sages. In fact, the Vedas are the oldest spiritual scriptures in the library of humanity. The ancient sages did not invent or create the teachings of the Vedas, rather, the Vedas are considered to be revealed teachings that were intuitively received by these great teachers in the depths of their meditative experiences.

Vedanta, which is the essence or culmination of the Vedas, describes Truth as one, non-dualistic, and absolute. Later, the sages elaborated on the content of the Vedas in the literature known as the Upanishads. But even these elaborations require interpretive guidance, if they are to be of practical utility to modern seekers. In this text, Pandit Rajmani explains the practical implications of these teachings to the modern student.

Meditation is the most powerful tool available to help those who are seeking to attain the experience of Truth. Meditation is the technique that helps a student go beyond the mire of delusion and conflict that arises in the mind, for Truth cannot be known with the mind itself. Only by stilling the mind and the senses and by learning to go beyond the mind can anyone know Truth. Many techniques can help students in the preliminary stages of their *sadhana*, and it is true that for many students, preparation of the body, mind, and personality are necessary to allow the full potential of meditation to be achieved. But ultimately, meditation is the most important and vital tool needed to attain that goal. Those who sincerely seek to make progress on the meditative path should make certain that they are engaged in an authentic process of meditation, taught by a genuine teacher who can assist them with their questions. In other books, the basic techniques of meditation and the steps necessary for the deepening of meditation are discussed. This volume is addressed mostly to those who are already embarked on the path of meditation and who want to further develop their understanding of their tradition.

Students of meditation will find that as they pursue this goal, many questions arise. At such times, they can call upon the guidance and assistance of those who have gone before them on the path. External guidance helps the student to make the connection with the Teacher within. I know that those who study and follow the guidance given in this book will receive assistance in deepening their practice of meditation and coming closer to the attainment of Truth. As Pandit Tigunait reminds the student, "the light of eternity dwells in the human body. By knowing the systematic yogic methods of penetrating your inner being, it is possible to reach the innermost core of this temple and attain the delight that lies within." May all who read this important book make progress on their spiritual journey.

1

Origin and Development of the Tradition

In reality, there is only one tradition, the tradition that includes all, and excludes none . . . . the tradition of truth. Truth is eternal and not influenced by time and place, nationality, or race. It remains undisturbed and independent of the whims of society and its transient fashions. It is without boundaries or limitations, and it is not confined to any particular geography or region.

Sincere seekers and teachers of the tradition of truth, likewise, are not bound by limitations of nationality; geography; or the fetters of personal ego, ignorance, attachment, aversion, or fear. In the light of these definitions, the tradition of the Himalayan masters refers not so much to a geographical identity as to a symbolic representation of the heights of spiritual wisdom.

In the present century, our best scientists have explored and studied nature as it exists outside of ourselves. Using their minds with utmost creativity, they have designed machines to examine all aspects of the external world—from the smallest microbes to distant galaxies. In millennia past, scientists (now known as the sages) focused the power and creativity of their minds on the inner space of their own beings, seeking to discover the full potential and nature of the human being. Using their finely trained, disciplined, and concentrated minds as their tool of exploration, they made discoveries in the laboratories of their own bodies and minds.

Human civilization is ancient, far beyond any recorded history, and has passed through many cycles of development and decline, so that even oral tradition gives us only sketchy information as to the chronological time when these sages lived and began their work.

Shankaracharya, the great yogi and philosopher, formally established the tradition of the Himalayan masters 1,200 years ago. However, the written record of this tradition first appears in the Vedic literature. The *Chhandogya Upanishad*, which was compiled in approximately 900 B.C., mentions an unbroken lineage of sages of more than 60 generations. Even if we assign only 25 years to each generation, this would take us back to the year 2400 B.C. According to oral tradition, the history of the lineage dates back at least 5,000 years and perhaps more than 10,000.

The lineage of the Himalayan sages is shrouded in mystery, especially in its earliest stages. Some of the ancient masters of the tradition have taught so many different disciplines to students over such a long span of time and are credited with having such extraordinary spiritual wisdom and power that it is difficult to believe that they were living human beings. These Himalayan masters were freethinkers, explorers of truth, and the architects of human civilization. It is as if they drew the blueprint of spirituality, and the philosophers, saints, and yogis who came later built and elaborated the structure on the basis of this blueprint.

Hundreds of shrines and holy places throughout the Himalayan region are dedicated to the memory of the sages, saints, and adepts who practiced and lived there. Thousands of years ago, this region seems to have had a more moderate climate than it does today. This climate supplied the sage-scientists with a perfect laboratory in which to carry out their experiments. The natural serenity, moderate temperatures, clean water, edible roots, fruit-laden trees, and comfortable dwellings far removed from worldly noise and distractions, provided the environment they needed for the subtle practices that made their discoveries possible.

Even now, as in the past, yogis belonging to this tradition go to the Himalayas for their higher training. If they are well prepared, they are able to join the cave monasteries that are hidden in the interiors of the Himalayan peaks. Mere curiosity is not enough to enable a person to gather his or her courage, begin the journey, reach the caves, receive instruction, and attain the highest state of spiritual illumination. The cave monasteries have their own kind of subtle fences that prevent half-hearted seekers from reaching them. The charms and temptations of the world, comfort-oriented tendencies of the mind, and ultimately, a lack of strong inspiration serve to screen the students. Only a fortunate few have the ability to take advantage of the rare opportunity to study with sages and to practice under their guidance.

Because the mountains cannot support large numbers of people, many of the problems related to overpopulation—such as possessiveness, greed, theft, violence, and fear—are virtually unknown there. The sages have used the hardships of mountain life to cultivate such spiritual virtues as non-possessiveness, generosity, love, and fearlessness.

This Himalayan way of life has remained unchanged. Villagers find great delight in sharing their limited resources with strangers. In fact, in their purity and innocence, they do not consider anyone to be a stranger and treat anyone who arrives at their door unexpectedly as a guest. This attitude and the simplicity of the people help yogis to survive in the Himalayas without carrying the burden of worldly possessions.

Ancient scriptures, such as the Vedas, the Upanishads, and the Puranas, are filled with descriptions of peaceful settings where the great sages spent their time. Such places are not found exclusively in the Himalayas. Many other mountain ranges and hills (such as the Vindhya Mountains, which stretch from central India all the way to the southern peninsula) also served as havens for spiritual seekers and teachers. However, changing weather patterns during the past millennia have made living conditions in these mountains harsher than they were in earlier times. Places such as Chitrakut in the northern Vindhya range; Nasik and Amarakantak in central India; Girnar near the west coast in Gujarat; and Arunachala in the south are still spiritually active centers. Ultimately, these sites are connected to the cave monasteries that lie deep in the Himalayas. Students from these centers are often sent to the caves for their higher training, and sometimes adepts from the cave monasteries travel to these places to guide the students in their practices.

From a literary point of view, the tradition of the Himalayan masters refers to the tradition that was expounded in the Vedas, and then gradually evolved while passing through the development of the Upanishads and the Puranas, all the way to the saintly literature written in the regional languages of India. Therefore, in essence, the tradition of the Himalayan masters is the tradition of the Vedic sages.

Narayana: The Primordial Sage

According to both oral and literary sources, Narayana is the founding sage of this tradition. He is believed to be one of the immortal, primordial sages who imparted wisdom to many saints and yogis.

Narayana transcends the confines of individual consciousness and has become one with universal consciousness. He is totally free from ignorance, ego, attachment, aversion, and fear; in him lies the seed of omniscience. This enlightened soul is also free from the karmas, fruits of karmas, and all the consequences that are brought about by the law of karma. He is the pure space of consciousness.

Just as the whole world exists in space, and yet space remains untouched by the world, so all other sages, adepts, and seekers dwell in Narayana, receive guidance from Narayana, and yet Narayana remains unaffected. Due to his elevated spiritual awareness, this sage is identified with the almighty God. The depth of spiritual awareness he dwells in is completely beyond the realm of time and space. Therefore, it can be said that Narayana is without a beginning and without an end. He existed and still exists, although no one knows whether or not he was ever born.

Because we are accustomed to locating the origin of an object, a person, a tradition, or an institution in space and time, it is difficult to accept that a figure such as Narayana and a tradition that "begins" with him is beginningless. We have become comfortable with the idea of the "beginning of creation" and the "end of creation." Therefore, we assume that any tradition that exists within this creation must have had a beginning. And that is why Narayana, who might well have been an actual person, is considered to be a mythological figure.

A peak named after Narayana stands amidst the majesty of the Himalayas. According to tradition, the famous shrine Badrinath is the site of Narayana's ashram. The spiritual practices he undertook while living in this ashram and the knowledge he imparted to numberless saints and sages are chronicled in the Vedic, tantric, and epic literature of India. The area around this shrine is now known as Badarikashram.

The Lineage

Sanatkumara is another sage who holds an exalted place in the history of the Himalayan masters. According to some sources, this sage and his other three brothers (Sanaka, Sanandana, and Sanatsujata) are the sons of Brahma, the Creator. According to other sources they are the offspring of a couple with the names of Ahimsa and Dharma. Whatever his parentage, Sanatkumara appears in the vast body of spiritual literature teaching the wisdom of the Vedas, Upanishads, yoga, and tantra. The unbroken lineage of the tradition that is discussed in this volume begins with this master. He is followed by Vashistha, Shakti, Parashara, Vyasa, Shuka Deva, Gaudapada, Govindapada, and Shankaracharya.

This list is not exhaustive—there were many other great saints and sages between Sanatkumara and Shankar-acharya, but it is difficult to pinpoint the order of their appearance. Some of these great sages are: Atharava, Angira, Daksinamurti, Chyavana, Dadhichi, Dattatreya, Hayagriva, Parashurama, and Haritayana. These sages are the seers of different mantras and the teachers of different spiritual sciences, such as *agni vidya*, the science of the spiritual sun; *chandra vidya*, the science of the spiritual moon; *deha vijnana*, the science pertaining to the subtle mysteries of the body; and *svara vijnana*, the science of breath.

The breadth and scope of spiritual literature that issued from the sages of the Himalayan tradition is enormous. In preparing the present volume, we were forced to be extremely selective. After some thought, we elected to include only the eight masters whose teachings have the most direct bearing on the questions that confront most serious seekers today. Accordingly, this volume contains chapters on

Tree of the Tradition

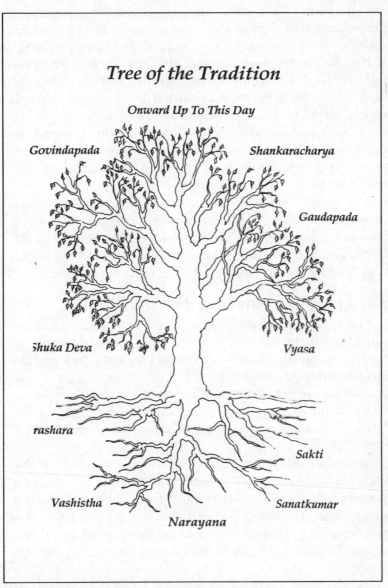

Onward Up To This Day

Govindapada

Shankaracharya

Gaudapada

Shuka Deva

Vyasa

rashara

Sakti

Vashistha

Sanatkumar

Narayana

Although the sages whose names appear here have been consistently mentioned in this order in the records of the lineage, there are numerous unnamed branches. No one other than the tree, the perennial source of wisdom, knows which branch grew first.

Sanatkumara, Vashistha, Dattatreya, Parashurama, and Shankaracharya. These five masters were either authors themselves or had students who recorded their teachings. Vyasa, who is the most famous of all the ancient masters— not only for his wisdom but also for the overwhelming volume of his writing—was excluded because his work is widely available. Many of the other great sages in this lineage, such as Atharava and Angira, contributed mainly to the esoteric aspect of yogic literature. The teachings imparted by these masters is of interest only to those who are whole-heartedly dedicated to mystical experiences.

The other three masters included in this volume— Vidyaranya Yati, Madhusudana Saraswati, and Swami Rama—are considerably more modern. They represent different facets of the unbroken lineage of sages that began with Shankaracharya and continues even until this day.

The Literary Sources of the Tradition

The Vedas and Upanishads are the most ancient literary sources of this tradition. Indeed, the Vedas are the oldest spiritual scriptures in the library of humanity and contain the wisdom revealed to the great saints and sages. These are not the works of an ordinary intellect but the spontaneous, intuitive revelations that came to the sages in the form of words. That is why every word and verse in the Vedas is called a mantra.

Later on, the sages elaborated on the content of the Vedas, explaining how to study and practice the mantras in daily life. Upanishadic literature was the result. In the Upanishads, the sages present the essence of the Vedas and describe yogic techniques of contemplation and meditation for studying both manifest and unmanifest aspects of reality.

Hundreds of Upanishads evolved from the Vedas, but eleven are considered major: Isha, Kena, Katha, Prashna, Mundaka, Mandukya, Chhandogya, Taittriya, Aitareya,

Brihadaranyaka, and Svetasvatara. These Upanishads expound the theory of *advaita*, the one absolute truth without a second. They remind aspirants to be aware of the absolute truth and aspire to attain it even while experiencing all the vicissitudes of life. In its opening verses, the *Isha Upanishad* conveys the message of the Vedic seers:

> This whole world has evolved from one absolute truth, Isha. The whole world, even after its manifestation, dwells in Isha; all worldly objects are a gift from Isha to human beings. Therefore, enjoy the objects of the world, but never get attached to them. Do not covet, do not possess, because nothing belongs to you. While performing your actions, desire to live for 100 years. Actions you perform while maintaining the awareness of Isha do not bind you.

Although the Upanishads contain references to highly evolved yogic practices, such references are too brief and compact to be understood without the help of an experienced master. However, the contemplative aspects of Upanishadic teachings are very systematic. That is why the eleven major Upanishads have served as a sourcebook for different philosophical systems and contemplative schools of spirituality.

The higher disciplines of yoga and meditation mentioned in the Vedas and Upanishads are fully explained in another group of texts known as the Tantras, or Agamas. But the tantric texts have a drawback—the contents are presented in an extremely symbolic and mystical language. Thus, if aspirants are to comprehend the true intent of these texts, they must be instructed directly by a master.

The outstanding tantric texts of the Himalayan tradition are: *Sanaka Samhita, Sanandana Samhita, Sanatkumara Samhita, Vashistha Samhita,* and *Sukha Samhita.* Unfortunately, none of these scriptures are extant. However, there are thousands of existing tantric scriptures based on these five texts. The most important among them are: *Parashurama Kalpa Sutra, Tripura Rahasya, Nitya Sodashi-karnamah, Rudrayamala,* and *Saundaryalahari*—along with its 41 commentaries. Except for the *Tripura Rahasya* and *Saundaryalahari* none of the major tantric texts have been translated into English.

In addition to these Vedic and tantric texts, there is a third body of literature—the Puranas. They describe the practices undertaken by the sages, the experience they gained, and the students to whom they imparted their knowledge. The Puranas are in the form of stories, so the teachings they contain are much simpler and more comprehensible than the teachings in the Vedic and tantric literature.

The drawback is that the content is diluted, and a reader finds the point of the story only after wading through lengthy stories. Furthermore, because these stories were told, retold, and presented in various ways to different audiences, elaborations and distortions were gradually introduced. This particular body of literature is like a great ocean. In order to retrieve the pearls from it, a student must first figure out where to dive and then learn to dive deep.

The Different Facets of the Teaching

To meet the needs of aspirants in different times and places, the sages imparted various levels of knowledge and did so in a variety of idioms. The result is that there are thousands of texts. In them, the sages taught a philosophy of life that ranges from dualistic to non-dualistic, from a materialistic to a completely spiritual worldview, and from a life oriented around the family to a life of ascetic practices.

Keeping both the vastness of the body of spiritual literature and the depth of the sages' knowledge in mind, no one can ever claim with authority that "This and this alone is what the sages teach." In order to avoid the mistake of confining the sages and their teachings to a narrow framework, it is helpful to remember the following story about Buddha and his students.

The Buddhist texts recount that Buddha's students used to quarrel among themselves, each claiming that what he had learned from the master was the only true teaching. Once when Buddha was walking through the forest with his students, he picked up a handful of leaves and asked, "Does my hand contain more leaves than there are in the rest of the forest?"

"No," the students replied. "It's obvious that you have only a few leaves in your hand, while the leaves in the forest are innumerable."

"So it is with the knowledge that I have imparted to a few students. I know much more than I have taught."

Like Buddha, the sages of the Upanishads also warn their students: "Practice only those teachings that are meaningful to you at this particular stage of your development. Leave the rest for further study and contemplation. In time, you may come to know the importance of those teachings and come to understand them."

Some revelations transcend all lower and partial perspectives. The knowledge of non-dual, absolute truth is one such revelation. Acquiring this knowledge is like climbing the highest peak of a mountain and seeing the panorama below. All sights that were visible from the lower elevations are included in this view. But from the summit, they do not look exactly as they did when the viewer was standing in the valley or part way up the mountain. So it is with the spiritual quest. At different stages of spiritual unfoldment, different revelations are valid and appropriate.

From a practical standpoint, all the sages—regardless of which philosophy they teach or which particular aspect of truth they expound—share some common values. These common values constitute the basic teachings of this tradition.

The Basic Teachings

All human beings need a code for living a healthy life without disturbing the well-being of their communities and society. The Sanskrit phrase for this is *acharah prathamo dharmah*. According to the sages, before committing oneself to any spiritual path one must create a healthy lifestyle. The basic guidelines for healthy living are cleanliness and purity. One who observes these principles may be said to be observing this code of conduct.

Cleanliness (or purity) is crucial if an individual is to create a healthy environment for his or her own growth, the growth of others, and the welfare of future generations. This principle must be observed on all levels of existence—physical, verbal, and mental.

By practicing physical cleanliness, we ensure our own good health and the purity of our environment. The same is true in the verbal realm. The pollution we create by telling lies and speaking negatively is far more injurious and lasting than the problems we cause by failing to keep our bodies or our physical environment clean. In turn, the damage caused by mental impurity—anger, hatred, jealousy, and greed—is far more injurious and long-lasting than the damage caused by verbal impurity.

All of the sages speak with one voice in stressing the importance of eating pure, fresh food, breathing fresh air, speaking the truth, and maintaining purity of thought. This constitutes a human being's basic dharma. This is called *acharah*, which literally means "healthy living." Failing to observe this basic dharma is not a sin, but creating or tolerating unsanitary conditions is damaging to your own health and that of others. This principle is the backbone of civilized society, just as the next principle, *ahimsa* (non-violence) is the backbone of spirituality.

Non-violence is humankind's highest dharma. (*Ahimsa paramo dharmah*.) Violence is the root of all vices. All species—human and non-human—are naturally inclined to peace and happiness. No one wants to be miserable. Therefore, causing pain to yourself or others violates both the law of nature and divine law.

Wherever there is conflict between ahimsa and our personal cultural values, customs, and religious practices, ahimsa must be preserved. Ahimsa can help resolve all conflicts between different religions and cultures. It is the only way to bring humanity into one fold and open the eyes of aspirants to the manifestation of one truth in all that exists.

Regardless of which path we choose, the physical body cannot be ignored. The body is the primary means of practicing dharma. (*Shariram adyam khalu dharamsadhanam.*) From a practical standpoint, the body is the basic vehicle for reaching the goal of life's journey. A sound mind dwells in a healthy body. An unhealthy body can create innumerable impediments. Those whose time and energy are consumed with solving problems created by the body have little opportunity to explore the higher levels of truth. Therefore, the lifestyle and practices that help maintain a healthy body are an integral part of *sadhana* (spiritual practice).

The body is the living shrine of the divine. (*Deho devalayah proktah.*) The light of eternity dwells in the human body. By knowing the systematic yogic method of penetrating your inner being, it is possible to reach the innermost core of this temple and experience the bliss that lies within. According to the sages, to be born as a human is a great opportunity. Failing to attain the highest realization before dropping the body is the greatest loss a human being can experience.

One must be fearless. Fear springs from duality. With the knowledge of non-dual truth, one attains immortality. (*Dvaitad vai bhayam bhavati advaitad vai amritah bhavanti.*) This is the central theme of the teachings of the Himalayan masters. Fear springs from the desire for self-preservation.

No matter how many systems of philosophy and psycho-therapy a human being applies, fear of death cannot be overcome unless a person realizes his or her unity with one, all-embracing, absolute truth. As long as an individual perceives himself or herself as an individual, that person remains afraid of losing this individuality.

The ego is the source of the sense of individuality. Although the ego is aware that it is a false self, it does not want to accept this fact. Thus, it creates conflict and fear. The knowledge of the absolute truth and our oneness with it is the ground on which fear vanishes completely. That is the goal of sadhana. The sages equate this state of fearlessness with the attainment of immortality.

External peace manifests from internal peace. (*Vyakter vai virat. Antas shantar bahis shantih.*) One can gather means and resources only from a peaceful external world. A person fully equipped with means and resources will encounter the fewest obstacles, and can advance on the spiritual path most easily.

According to the tradition of the Himalayan masters, each individual is a vessel of light. If humankind is to live in peace and harmony, this light must radiate from each of us. The relationship between individuals and humanity is like the relationship between the trees and the forest. Just as a large group of trees collectively creates a forest, so individuals form families, communities, societies, and humanity.

At first glance, it may not be apparent that the health of the forest deteriorates when individual trees are diseased, but it is impossible to have a healthy forest without healthy trees. In the same way, it is impossible to have a healthy society unless the individuals who make up the society are healthy.

That is why the Himalayan masters emphasize the enlightenment and self-transformation of individuals. As the individual's quality of life improves, the quality of life of the society also improves. A prosperous society supplies the means for living comfortably. People who are comfortable have a better chance of exploring and understanding the subtle truths of life. Thus, this entire cycle of spiritual unfoldment begins and ends with the individual.

All of the ethical, moral, and social values of the sages are based on one spiritual truth: There is only one Brahman without a second. (*Eko Brahma dvitiyo nasti.*) "Overcome all differences within and without" is the message of the sages.

Like different steps on a ladder, all the paths gradually lead to the same truth. (*Tadunmukhah sarvapanthanah sopanavata.*) Before climbing energetically toward the goal, it is of the utmost importance for an aspirant to find where he or she is on the ladder. Each aspirant must stand firm in his or her own sadhana and avoid the mistake of unnecessarily judging which particular step on the ladder—which particular path—is higher or lower, superior or inferior. Such an attitude helps the aspirant rise above the apparent contradictions among the different paths.

Experience the Atman within—this is indeed immortality. (*Atmanyevatmanam nivodhata tadeva amaratvam.*) This is the sages' most important message to us. Searching for truth in the external world is not only a waste of time; it is also a source of endless misery. If you cannot find your Self wherever you are, then certainly you cannot find your Self anywhere else. Not finding your Self is called death, and finding your Self is called immortality.

The Faces of Truth

Truth is one, but its faces are many. Depending on their inclinations and perspectives, and those of their students, the sages revealed different faces of the truth at different times, describing it while standing on different platforms. Just as different faces of the truth are equally valid and authentic, so are the different teachings of the sages, which contain various grades and degrees of revelation. The chapters that follow are meant to present the faces of the truth that are most relevant to the seeker in the present age.

2

Sanatkumara

The teachings and spiritual techniques that the great sage, Sanatkumara, shared with aspirants have been preserved in a variety of works, among them the *Chhandogya Upanishad*, the *Mahabharata, Harivamsa Purana, Vamana Purana, Skanda Purana, Brahmanda Purana*, and the *Mahatymya Khanda of Tripura Rahasyam*. Information about this sage also appears in the writings of prominent scholars who contributed articles to the multi-volume publication, *Kalyana* (which has not been translated into English). The teachings, presented here in the form of a dialogue between Sanatkumara and Narada, are taken primarily from the *Chhandogya Upanishad*.

Narada's Dilemma

Once there was a learned yogi named Narada. In addition to his knowledge of the scriptures and spiritual disciplines, he was expert in philosophy, history, grammar, mathematics, economics, ethics, logic, mythology, astrology, astronomy, medicine, and a host of other disciplines. He had mastered sixty-four different branches of art and science. His students revered him for his knowledge and he was recognized everywhere as a person of highest wisdom.

But one day he began to have second thoughts about his accomplishments. As Narada pondered his true Self, he not only began re-evaluating his way of life, but also his wisdom. He realized that he wasn't truly happy, even though he taught others the art of happiness.

Narada pondered this and concluded that the methods that he taught for removing frustration, dejection, depression, and loneliness could not really help students if they did not help the teacher. He was not happy, despite his abundant knowledge in a variety of subjects. He found this bewildering. And what of others whose knowledge was much more limited than his? How could they be happy? As he considered this, he began to wonder if anyone in the world was happy.

The more he thought about it, the more he became determined to find true happiness. Not knowing what else to do, he handed all his responsibilities over to his senior students and set out on a quest. He was greeted with honor wherever he went, but although he expressed his doubts and spoke of his search, no one took him seriously. People thought he was simply being humble, so no one offered to help.

Sanatkumara Enlightens Narada

Finally, Narada met Sanatkumara and asked the great sage to help him attain happiness and direct his energies to the attainment of the highest truth. Sanatkumara agreed to help and asked Narada what he had already learned. Narada went over the long list of arts and sciences that he had mastered and had been successfully teaching others. When he finished listing his accomplishments, the following dialogue transpired:

Sanatkumara: You know so much and still you are not happy with yourself.

Narada: My knowledge has not brought me peace or joy. It does not help me overcome my fear of death, and thus its value is compromised. I'm tired of knowing and drowning in misery. Take me beyond knowing to where I may find freedom.

Everything I have learned so far seems to be a means of exercising my skills or gaining worldly recognition. How can the knowledge I have obtained through years of arduous study have any real value when I will lose it at death and have to start all over again in the next lifetime?

Sanatkumara: The problem is that you confuse true knowledge, which is gained directly from within, with mere information, which is gained through words and sentences. All the branches of art and science that you mentioned are mere collections of words—they have no substance. You learned them in the form of words, and you pass them on to your students in the form of words.

Your knowledge of these disciplines gave you the means of maintaining your existence on this earthly plane, which is why most people master these subjects. It is the nature of our economy that some are employed as teachers and others are students, even though what they are teaching and learning fails to bring true happiness.

But the book of life remains unread, and the part of you that is destined to unveil the mystery of life prompts you to open this book and read attentively. While you are engaged in mundane activities, you are ignoring the call of the soul. Thus, you create a ground for inner conflict. This inner conflict, which arises from ignoring the soul's constant reminder of the goal of life, results in frustration, destroying your peace and happiness.

You may be able to hide yourself from the rest of the world, but you cannot conceal yourself from yourself, from your inner soul. Without achieving true happiness from within, you cannot convince yourself that you have found peace without. The only way to achieve real peace

This image of the sage Narada has been drawn on the basis of his characteristic of parama bhakti, the highest state of divine love and ecstasy attributed to him in the Puranas.

and happiness is to know yourself at every level.

Narada: How can I know myself at every level?

Sanatkumara: Your speech is a reflection of your thoughts. Your inner life is created by the way you think. If you want to know your inner life, first examine your speech. The more you study your speech, the more the contents of your mind are revealed. Study the connection between speech and mind, and you will find that speech is the means through which the mind expresses itself.

By observing silence, you can attain some degree of control over your speech, but this will not bring you peace and happiness. Once the disturbance at the level of speech is quieted, you will notice unexpected turbulence in the mind.

In order to attain peace, you must work systematically. First, bring peace to your tongue. This means speaking sweetly and making sure that you do not harm either yourself or others through your speech. Avoid meaningless talk. These observances will lead you to mental peace. By observing this discipline of speech, you maintain awareness of Brahman—the highest truth. Practicing Brahman awareness helps you create and maintain an environment of *satsanga*, the company of the wise.

The next step is to study your mind, for mind is subtler than speech: contemplate on what you think, why you think, and how your thoughts affect your speech and actions. If you cannot quiet the mental noise, then fill your mind with Brahman consciousness.

While trying to understand your mind and attempting to fill it with Brahman consciousness, you will notice an even subtler force called *samkalpa*, the power of determination. The mind cannot think unless you decide what it will think. At your behest, your mind thinks, and only when your mind thinks do the words come forward. The power of determination, which is a subtle desire springing from the core of your being, is the driving force behind the activities of your mind.

Narada: If samkalpa, the power of determination, is even more subtle than the mind, then why can't we make our minds do what we want them to do? Furthermore, it seems that we have very little control over our samkalpa and, thus, the mind's activities go unchecked.

Sanatkumara: You are right, Narada. Your samkalpa is affected by the subtle impressions of the past and by thought, speech, and actions that you have stored in the *chitta*, the mindfield. Because you have forgotten the subtle impressions of the past, as well as the place where you stored them, they become unconscious; thus, the storehouse is called the unconscious mind. The material in the unconscious mind affects your samkalpa outside of your conscious awareness. In turn, your samkalpa loses control over the conscious part of the mind.

For example, sometimes you think thoughts you don't want to think, speak words you don't wish to speak, and perform actions that you do not want to perform. Or you postpone certain thoughts or actions. All this is due to the unconscious.

Narada: These unconscious impressions in the mind seem to be completely autonomous. Is there any rule governing how and when the subtle impressions of the past arise?

Sanatkumara: Contemplation awakens these subtle impressions. Without thought as an instigating factor, they cannot become active. The law is simple: Similar attracts similar. Nothing is totally unconscious. The unconscious mind cannot function if part of it is not conscious in some way. Therefore, your conscious thinking, which you may call contemplation, triggers corresponding *samskaras*, subtle impressions of the past, which, in turn, affect your samkalpa and your conscious mind, as well as your speech and action.

Beyond the conscious mind, all other principles—such as samkalpa, the unconscious mind and, ultimately, this power of contemplation—gradually become more subtle. For a novice, it is hard to work at the level of contemplation. In this context, contemplation means to dive into the depths of your thinking process. You must aim to penetrate the nature of the unconscious mind.

Contemplation prevents the unconscious mind from controlling the conscious mind. However, it is your *samkalpa shakti* that makes contemplation effective. This power of decision is more powerful than the unconscious mind.

Remember, Narada, all the subtle impressions of the past stored in the unconscious mind lie dormant there. Unless something awakens them, these samskaras have no power to affect either your determination or your conscious mind.

First, you make a decision and then based on that, you contemplate. Implementation of your ideas comes later. Contemplation is far more subtle than actually performing a task. Before executing a task, a decision has to be made. That process of deciding is affected by your previous experiences. Before the force of contemplation triggers the power of determination and reaches the conscious mind, it awakens the unconscious material. Thus, in a sense, the unconscious and the other faculties of our inner being—such as the power of determination and the conscious mind—become active simultaneously. Therefore, Narada, from the very beginning contemplate on the principle that is contrary to your negative samskaras.

Because it is hard to penetrate these subtle layers of our being in the early stages of our *sadhana*, it is advisable to fill our contemplation with Brahman consciousness, while simultaneously working toward self-transformation and self-improvement.

The power to contemplate on truth, which is conducive to peace and happiness, springs from the knowledge of the truth. Unless we know the antidote for the negative samskaras, we cannot begin to contemplate such principles. Therefore, knowledge is more subtle than the contemplation itself. I am not speaking of intellectual knowledge, but of self-revealed, intuitive knowledge. This knowledge does not come from books, discourses, or reasoning. You maintain Brahman consciousness by keeping the highest goal in mind throughout your study of the scriptures, through your discourses, and in your reasoning. As a result, the lower knowledge that you gain through worldly sources becomes a means of gaining the knowledge of the highest truth.

Narada: All these years I thought that I had a goal. I believed that the way I was studying and teaching was a definite method of *svadhyaya*, self-study.

Sanatkumara: Your studies and teaching activities were a means of entertaining yourself, of gaining recognition, of finding some intellectual satisfaction, and of keeping yourself busy and earning a living. Such studying and teaching is mere action. No one can achieve freedom through action.

Narada: Without knowing what else to do, should I abandon all these actions? Aren't these actions better than many other actions? Aren't they better than not performing any actions at all?

Sanatkumara: That's not the point, Narada. It's a matter of gathering your courage and tapping your inner strength. Mere knowledge regarding action or inaction is of no use. Your resolve to act works only if it is accompanied by inner strength. Gather that inner strength. Such strength comes, not from the surface of your mind or from your intellect, but from the depth of your soul. Only such inner strength is unalloyed and divine. You will persist and accomplish your task only with the help of inner strength, which you may call the divine force—*shakti*. Without shakti, the knowledge about action and the resolve to act will come to nothing.

Make your knowledge functional. Unless it is functional, knowledge is a burden. Knowledge that doesn't wake you up and make you move forward is dead. Knowledge must be active and vibrant. It is from the womb of active knowledge that the power of action is born. Knowledge derives its life from the unrestricted power of will. This unrestricted power of will is known as *iccha shakti*.

Iccha shakti is the intrinsic characteristic of the highest truth, the supreme consciousness. This iccha shakti is also *kama kala*—initial or primordial, divine desire. Therefore, to make your knowledge active and vibrant, you must meditate and thereby unfold the supreme power of will within. The power of will, the power of knowledge, and the power of action go together.

Narada: How can I understand the nature of shakti and unfold that force within?

Sanatkumara: This primordial, divine force manifests in all the diverse names and forms that you perceive. If you want to attain a full understanding of that, you must understand the subtle mysteries of food.

Before a living organism evolves, food must exist to sustain it. First, comes the food; then, the organism. The life force is in both the food and the organism. Thus, the life force is both consuming and consumed. Unless you know who the consumer is and who is being consumed, you will never overcome the fear of death. Unless you know the intrinsic nature of the life force within you and within the objects that nourish you, you live with the fear that you will be unable to sustain your life.

There are two forms of fear—the fear of not having enough to maintain yourself and the fear of being consumed by the objects you possess. In either case, you remain involved with objects—either in acquiring those that make you feel secure or in ridding yourself of those that threaten you.

It is not enough to know that you need solid food, water, light, heat, and air to live. You must also know what it is that you actually receive from these things. How is the life force different from these things, and why is the life force supplied through them? Ultimately, you need to know under what conditions you receive and assimilate (or fail to receive and/or assimilate) the life force from these substances. At this point, Narada, the inquiry moves across the boundary of physics and into the realm of metaphysics, or even into pure spiritual science. The nature and structure of the universe, its functioning forces, and its constituent components are thoroughly studied in the science of shrividya.

Sanatkumara explained this science in detail in the prominent text on shrividya, Sanatkumara Samhita. In it, the sage leads Narada, step-by-step, unveiling the mysteries of the power of memory and its connection with the principles of hope, pranic energy, the power of decisiveness, faith, conviction and, ultimately, happiness. Sanatkumara stresses that true happiness cannot be limited by time, space, and causation. True happiness cannot be compared with any experience at all. It cannot be put in the categories like "less and more," "small and big," or "short-lived and long-lasting."

Sanatkumara: You have come from bliss, Narada, and no matter how much you get lost in the world, part of you remains aware of your blissful nature. It's that part that reminds you, from within, to attain eternal, boundless bliss and to become one with it.

The urge to attain happiness is the driving force behind all pursuits in life. Because of the charms and temptations of worldly objects, you think that you don't have enough time to turn inward and find happiness within yourself. This frightens and frustrates you. On the other hand, you miss that happiness, and in order to rid yourself of that feeling of "missingness," you try to find happiness in the external world.

Before you undertake a task, there is the light of hope. That hope itself gives you some degree of joy. Hoping to find happiness by obtaining objects, you work hard, all the while telling yourself that you are very happy to be working. When you obtain an object, you may feel delighted for a moment, but that delight is soon replaced with dissatisfaction. And so you look for something else. In this way, you go on performing your actions in the external world with the elusive hope that the next action will make you happy, even though the last one did not. Every experience you have of failure to find satisfaction is a lesson. It teaches you that there is no real happiness in the external world. But your own insecurity and skepticism about finding happiness in the unknown inner realm, possibly at the price of losing the pleasure of the external world, frightens you. Your attachment to worldly objects and your ignorance about the infinite wealth within is the source of all fears. Fear and happiness never co-exist. As long as you have no direct experience of the wealth of happiness that lies within you, you must trust the experiences of the sages and find the courage to turn the mind inward.

Resolving to find the happiness within solely on the basis of the experiences of the sages or the testimony of the scriptures is called "standing on the ground of faith." Before you gain direct experience of the truth within, faith is the only force that can loosen the fetters of desire and attachment to worldly pleasure. Faith is higher knowledge in its own right. It gives you the courage to turn away from the external world and find the truth in the place where all limitation ends.

Narada: In practical terms, how do I begin my search?

Sanatkumara: You begin with food. Through *ahara shuddhi*, by eating pure food, you purify your body. Then, just as your gross body needs solid food to maintain its existence, your pranic body needs pranic energy to sustain itself. Senses, mind, ego, and intellect all require their own kind of food.

Sattvic food, which is fresh, light, and nutritious, taken in the appropriate quantities, at the right time, and with the right attitude of mind, provides a pure diet. Similarly, breathing clean air, with a regulated dominance of right and left nostrils, nourishes the pranic body. Maintaining positive thoughts in a cheerful mind provides nutritious food to the mental body. Constant awareness of the fact that anything indicated by the words "my" and "mine" belongs to *prakriti*—whereas the truth indicated by "I" is pure conscious-ness—supplies nutritious food to the ego. Purify yourself by maintaining the constant awareness that all objects belong to nature and that it is a mistake to identify with them. Simi-larly, remaining aware of your pure existence, conscious-ness, and bliss is the way to supply food to the *anandamaya kosha*, the body made of bliss.

By creating a bridge between different aspects of our being and strengthening rather than weakening each of these aspects, we attain perfect realization of the Self. Know yourself at every level and find yourself perfect in every respect. That is the only way to attain true happi-ness.

You purify your external and internal life by purifying the food you provide to every level of your being. As a result, your memory becomes sharp and stable; then you begin to glimpse your inner Self and eventually come to know it well. As these glimpses of your inner Self become brighter and steadier, your attachment to worldly objects and desires for pleasure becomes thinner and weaker. The weaker your desires and attachments, the fewer obstructions they create to the illumination of your inner Self. And the fewer obstructions in the light that radiates from within, the brighter you will see yourself both within and without.

By imparting this knowledge, Sanatkumara removed all Narada's questions regarding worldly and spiritual knowl-edge and external and internal life, and thus helped him attain freedom from the frustration caused by "missingness" and loneliness.

This dialogue between Sanatkumara and Narada is just a fragment of the sage's teachings, which are documented in the vast literature of the Upanishads and Puranas, and later, in the Agamas and Tantras. In the more accessible literature, Sanatkumara is portrayed as "paramahansa," the highest grade *jnani* (knower of truth), perfectly and eternally established in the principle of *vairagya* (non-attachment). He is *brahmarishi*, the knower of Brahman, who guides the prepared students on the path of knowledge.

On one hand, his body is made of pure light and descends in the pure mindfield of the yogis, imparting the highest wisdom. On the other hand, to those who have not reached the high degree of purity acquired through yoga and, thus, are unable to face the brilliance that emanates from his presence, he materializes himself in human form and lovingly guides them on the path of truth, usually through *bhakti* yoga, the path of devotion.

In tantric literature, Sanatkumara is the primordial master, from whom flows the wisdom of tantra, especially the wisdom of the ten *mahavidyas*—the sublime paths of shakti-oriented tantric practices. In the splendid tree of the tradition of the sages, Sanatkumara is like the root and the others are like the trunk and the branches.

3

Vashistha

As legend has it, Vashistha is the son of Brahma, the creator of the universe. It happened like this: Brahma noticed numberless individual souls living in the darkness of ignorance. Their existence was miserable, and they seemed unable to overcome their grief. These helpless souls, exhausted from the strenuous round of worldly activities, simply fell asleep at the end of each lifetime, hoping to get some rest and awaken to find their troubles at an end. But that never happened, and they remained caught in the cycle of death and rebirth.

Seeing this, Brahma said to himself, "Let me bring forth my beloved son who has the wisdom to help these suffering souls."

Instantly Vashistha emerged, radiant as the midday sun. Bowing his head in reverence to Brahma, he asked, "What would you have me do, Creator of the world?"

"Beloved son, I command you to descend to the world and, while living as a human, show those who are entangled in the cycle of worldly transmigration the path of freedom and enlightenment."

Vashistha responded, "This manifest world, myself included, is part of the divine game. This process of creation and annihilation goes on under the guidance of the supreme force, *maha maya*. The illusory concept of bondage and liberation is superimposed on all individuals, although in truth it has no meaning. How can the true essence of the soul ever be bound and miserable? Attaining freedom and overcoming misery is simply an illusion."

Brahma realized that because His son's perfection and purity had not been compromised by worldly afflictions, he had difficulty understanding bondage and freedom, pleasure and pain, and sorrow and happiness. He also remembered that because His son was an omniscient soul, he was able to see the essential nature of omniscience and bliss, his own Self, and the Self of all. In the light of his unsurpassed omniscience he was unable to see the darkness of ignorance and the misery it caused. His omniscience would have to be taken from him if he were to understand human consciousness and find practical methods of helping humans overcome their pain and misery. With this thought, Brahma spoke: "May you lose your omniscience, my son."

Vashistha's omniscience vanished instantly. He wondered who he was. He did not even recognize his own father. With sorrow and fear, he asked, "Can you tell me who I am?"

"You are Vashistha, my son."

"Then who are you, sir?" asked Vashistha.

"I am Brahma, your father, and the Creator of the universe."

"How unfortunate I am," said Vashistha. "You say I am your son, and yet I do not know whose son I am. You are my father, and yet I do not know in what sense you are my father. I find myself a human being, completely separate from you, with none of your qualities or characteristics. Help me, Father. Save me! Show me the path of security and protection. Let me understand my purpose and how I may accomplish it."

Honoring this request, Brahma explained the nature of ignorance, step-by-step, finally reintroducing Vashistha to his pure Self, wherein lies the seed of unsurpassed omniscience and bliss. Then Vashistha humbly bowed his head and said, "How may I serve you?"

"Go to the earth, beloved Vashistha, and teach your fellow beings to recognize and follow the path that best suits them."

That is how the human race came to be blessed with the presence of Vashistha. According to the scriptures, this sage lived for a long time. He both practiced and taught almost all the spiritual disciplines during his long life's journey. The following episode from his spiritual practice describes what peace is and where it can be found.

Vashistha Learns a Lesson About Finding Peace

Once, Vashistha decided to abandon the rush and roar of the world and find a place free from all noise. He set off for one of the far-distant galaxies where he was unknown. Traveling through the vast abyss of space, he went past the boundaries of this three-dimensional world and reached a place where an entirely new universe began.

There in pure space—far from planets and stars—he hoped to remain undisturbed. He sat down to begin his meditation, and went into deep *samadhi*. After several hundred years passed, he opened his eyes and was amazed to see a beautiful woman walking toward him.

"A living human being here in empty space? What is this?" he wondered.

The woman approached, paid her homage, and pleaded, "Help me, Oh son of Brahma."

"Who are you, young maiden, and what can I do for you?" Vashistha inquired.

"I am the daughter of the creator of a galaxy. Although I am in the full flower of my youth, my father will not allow me to marry. Please talk to him. I'm sure he will listen to you. Prevent my youth from being wasted."

Vashistha agreed to accompany her to her father's galaxy, and so they set out. When they arrived, the creator of that galaxy came forward and received Vashistha respectfully. After the two had exchanged greetings, Vashistha asked, "Why will you not allow your daughter to marry?"

Her father replied, "In seven days this entire galaxy and everyone in it, myself included, will be destroyed. I have told her to make the best use of these seven days and attain that immortal knowledge which remains unaffected by the forces of creation and destruction. Why create a bond for the sake of pleasure that is destined to last only for seven days?"

Vashistha turned to the woman and said, "Your father is right. Why do you want to concentrate on momentary enjoyment, which is bound to end in misery?"

"All living beings adjust their minds and hearts to the idea of pleasure and pain," she replied. "The intensity of longing and fulfillment of a person whose life lasts only seven days is qualitatively the same as that of a person whose life spans 700 years. How can you apply the standard of inner happiness and spiritual bliss of an enlightened person like yourself to someone who is completely affected by the turmoil of sensory and psychological longing? Is it fair to force me to remain dissatisfied and unfulfilled for the remaining seven days of my life?"

The young woman urged her father and the sage to look at things from her perspective. Vashistha thought about it thoroughly and concluded that the principles of knowledge and non-attachment—and even the idea of enlightenment itself—cannot be imposed from outside; knowledge must manifest from within. The powerful drive of worldly desires must be acknowledged and transformed. If aspirants are to start smoothly, continue safely, and reach the goal of enlightenment peacefully, they must not fight their natural urges. Thus, Vashistha advised the young woman to get married and enjoy the pleasures she was seeking while remaining aware of how transitory and superficial those pleasures are. He explained that constant awareness of the unsatisfactory nature of worldly pleasures and a natural longing to attain eternal peace and joy within can help a person gain freedom from worldly desires and become established in the real Self.

The story goes on to tell how Vashistha stayed to witness the destruction of the galaxy. This experience of leaving the earth, meditating in empty space, encountering the young woman, and witnessing the destruction of a galaxy, led Vashistha to re-evaluate his concept of peace and the means of attaining it. He concluded that mind can fill even empty space and create a crowd even in a void. Afterward, he wondered if all that he witnessed had actually happened. He had nothing but the mind itself to verify what had occurred. This experience and his mind's failure to grasp the truth—its inability to know for certain what was real—led him to doubt that the world we live in is real. As a result, he expounded the philosophy of reflectionism.

Vashistha's Philosophy of Reflectionism

According to the philosophy of reflectionism, which in Sanskrit is known as *abhasa vada* or *pratibimba vada*, this universe of ours is only a projection of the mind. The world has no essence of its own—the mind simply projects its contents and then believes that these projections are real. A strong belief in the validity of worldly objects brings a sense of stability. The stronger the belief in the world, the longer that world lasts. The moment the mind sees its own tricks—its projection and its firm belief in the objects it has created—this entire make-believe structure vanishes. Thus, this world is merely a creation of the mind.

This is also the case with internal states, such as peace and happiness. First, the mind creates a condition of dissatisfaction and then lets itself believe that it is miserable.

Once it realizes it is miserable, it cannot be happy until it has overcome this misery. And that is how this tricky mind begins its peace pilgrimage. The farther it walks on its pilgrimage, the more miserable it becomes until, one day, either someone reminds the mind or it remembers by itself. At that point, the thinking process goes something like this:

"Oh mind, there is no shrine of peace outside you. Change the direction of your journey and find peace within.

"In order to turn inward, you must first transcend your own belief system—the belief that someone else will give you salvation, that someone else will make you happy. In order to find peace, oh mind, first you must overcome your habit of tricking yourself—making your own projections and then getting entangled in them.

"Make yourself simple. Learn to be quiet rather than hyperactive. Do not mistake peace for an object that you attain. Rather, understand that peace is a mental state. That mental state is always present. However, mind, through your own self-created noise you disturb that state of stillness, which is called peace. Only you yourself can remove that disturbance."

The complete inner dialogue that Vashistha had with his mind is beautifully narrated by Valmiki in the *Yoga Vashistha*. This work is a treasure house of Vashistha's spiritual experiences, which he shared with his beloved student Rama, a prince who came to study with him at an early age. After completing his education, Rama returned home but soon fell into a deep depression. His father once again sought Vashistha's wise counsel. Vashistha advised Rama to visit the holy places and learn from the saints and yogis.

After several years of wandering, Rama gained a little peace of mind. Because he was not fully satisfied, he returned to live in Vashistha's ashram. On many different occasions, this enlightened sage and his fully prepared student discussed those issues that every sincere aspirant faces sooner or later. The following dialogue is a sample of an exchange between master and disciple.

The Problem of Mind

Rama: What should one do to unveil the subtle mysteries of life and attain peace and happiness?

Vashistha: Mind is the greatest of all mysteries. It stands between an individual and the highest truth and is the cause of both bondage and liberation. Properly trained, mind can help you attain enlightenment, but if misguided, it can leave you stranded on the shoals of confusion and bondage. Peace is created by the mind, Rama. First, make the decision to be content in any circumstance. From that womb of contentment, peace is born. It is foolish to expect to achieve peace by retiring into the deep forest or leaving for a distant galaxy. Ultimately, one must find peace within.

Rama: Why does the mind prefer to run in the external world rather than turning inward to find peace?

Vashistha: The mind has bound itself tightly to the senses. Driven by sense cravings, the mind runs to the external world. As long as you do not know how to withdraw the senses from the external world, you have almost no choice but to let your mind remain a victim of sense pleasure.

The objects of the senses, as well as the pleasure derived from them, are momentary. After experiencing a sensory pleasure, the mind realizes the emptiness of the experience. But, not knowing where else to find satisfaction, it turns again to the external world. Thus, dissatisfaction becomes a way of life. The constant failure to experience joy leads to frustration. Peace is lost, and the inner world becomes chaotic. Inner discontentment, frustration, and restlessness then manifest in a person's external life, and both internal and external worlds become full of misery.

Rama: What is the solution?

Vashistha: *Vairagya*—non-attachment—is the only way to overcome this strife. A person cultivates an attitude of non-attachment when she or he comes to realize that all the objects of the world are transitory. The value of worldly objects is simply a creation of the mind. Once you realize that you arrived in this world with nothing and will depart with nothing, you will not be attached to the objects of the world.

Rama: I know this is true but somehow I fail to maintain this knowledge, especially when it comes to interacting with the world.

Vashistha: This is because the mind is fully convinced that this world and its objects are real; this is called *maya*. Maya is a strong belief in the existence of that which does not exist. To illustrate this point, let me tell you a story.

Once a washerman asked his son to go to the barn and get his donkey. But when the son tried to fetch the donkey, he wouldn't budge. The boy went to his father and told him the donkey wouldn't move.

"Is the donkey tied up?" the washerman asked.

"No. That's what I don't understand," the son replied.

"Well then, slap him on the rump to get him moving!" the father replied in exasperation.

The son tried this but the donkey still wouldn't move. He went back to his father and said, "Father, he must be sick. Please come and see for yourself."

This time, father and son went together to fetch the donkey. The father also tried to get the donkey to move, but to no avail. Then suddenly, he understood the problem. He took the donkey's rope, which was attached to his halter but not attached to the post. He first wound the rope around the post and then unwound it and began walking out of the barn. Only then did the donkey follow him.

This, Rama, is the case with people whose minds are

fully convinced of the reality of worldly objects and the bondage they create. This world is not capable of binding either mind or soul; the mind is in bondage simply because it believes that it is in bondage.

Rama: How can the mind overcome this illusion?

Vashistha: The mind must apply a two-fold method. First, it must overcome its craving for worldly objects with the help of constant contemplation on the illusory nature of worldly pleasure. Second, the mind must recognize its true nature and maintain that awareness constantly.

Forgetfulness of the true nature of the Self is what makes a human being subject to timidity, weakness, fear, and insecurity. It is this forgetfulness that causes us to keep searching for a haven in the external world. Once you realize your inner Self, you become free from the charms of the world, as well as from the fear of death. I will tell you another ancient tale to illustrate this point.

Once there was a lion cub who was separated from the pride right after birth, before his eyes had opened. Thus he never saw his real mother. He was helpless, but after a few days a flock of sheep happened by. He joined the flock and was raised with the lambs. As a result, he identified himself with the sheep and learned to behave like them. He learned to follow others blindly, to be afraid of dogs, and to submit when whipped by the shepherd. He grew to full adulthood, but because he constantly watched the sheep who surrounded him, and because his identification with them was complete, he never noticed how big he was or what sharp, powerful claws he had. He never found out how fast he could run, how high he could jump, and how loud he could roar.

One day, another lion crept up on the flock and let out a tremendous roar. The flock scattered. The young lion, who was as frightened as the other sheep, ran away too. In full flight, he passed a pond and saw his reflection for the first time. To his astonishment, his reflection resembled the lion he was running from. He was confused. Why didn't he look like the other sheep? As he examined this reflection, he was disappointed at first because he expected to see a sheep, but his disappointment quickly turned into curiosity. As an experiment he tried roaring like the lion he had just heard and found that he could! This filled his mind with delight and wonder. He jumped and roared and relished the realization that he was truly a lion. He never returned to the flock, but joined the pride and lived as the king of the forest.

You see, Rama, through our identification, we create a self-image and, based on that, we create a reality. If this identification is false, we become victims of falsehood. If the identification is correct, then we are fortunate enough to live in the light of truth.

Rama: I understand, Gurudeva. Overcoming the charms and temptations of the world, turning the mind inward, and attaining a true glimpse of oneself is possible through vairagya—non-attachment. But the essence of vairagya is too subtle to grasp. Furthermore, while trying to practice vairagya, how do I deal with my other weaknesses, which distract me during *sadhana*?

Vashistha: Learn to withdraw your senses and mind systematically before practicing vairagya or committing yourself to any intense practice of contemplation or meditation. This process is called *pratyahara*—sense withdrawal.

Taming the Senses and Taming the Mind

People who search for joy in the external world are always disappointed. Desires and cravings begin in the mind and motivate the senses to contact objects. That is why trying to control the senses alone will not be effective.

The first step is to convince the mind and senses that it is necessary to withdraw. To do this, you must find out why the mind is running in the external world. You will discover that the mind and senses keep busy in the external world—or resort to sleep—in order to escape from reality, which is painful. This external search for peace is very tiring and, sooner or later, the mind stops to rest. Rest feels good. If the mind can be made to see and acknowledge the effect of rest, it will begin developing a willingness to rest and withdraw the senses.

When we pull in the mind and senses voluntarily with the thread of knowledge, we experience true relaxation. After the mind experiences the joyful stillness in the body that results from pratyahara, it can be successfully instructed to look within for the true source of happiness.

There are three ways of practicing pratyahara. The first is to withdraw the senses and mind from the external world, and then focus them consciously on a chosen object in the realm of the mind. Another way to practice is to see everything in the world as existing within the *Atman*—the Self. With this approach, nothing is outside the Atman, so there is no need to withdraw the senses. A third practice is to carry out all your activities as if they were sacred duties. In this way you bring sanctity to even the most mundane aspects of life. When a human being gives up all desires of the mind and delights in the Self, then he or she is said to be a person of steady wisdom.

If you cannot control your senses immediately, Rama, don't be discouraged. The process by which the senses move toward their objects is very subtle. It begins with thinking—you become attached to something just by thinking about it. Something becomes attractive because of inner cravings, or because of latent impressions from the past that exist in the mind. The *samskaras* and *vasanas* in the mind see something similar to themselves in the external objects and feel great joy in this correspondence. The inner experience of full identification is called enjoyment. In that affinity or feeling of sympathy you say, "This belongs to me." Attachment follows that thought.

Therefore, attachment arises from merely thinking

about something. The desire to act is based on that attachment. If something impedes that action, we become angry.
If we find that the obstruction cannot be overcome, we
become depressed. Or if we feel strong, we might fight the
obstruction. That produces anger. From anger, delusion
arises and, from that, loss of memory. With loss of
memory, the power of discrimination (*buddhi*) is lost. It is
then impossible to decide anything appropriately and, at
this point, a human being is doomed.

Study yourself, Rama, because only then can you build
the foundation needed to withdraw your senses and mind.
Look at the nature of pleasure and pain and determine for
yourself the results of attachment to the world of names
and forms. As a human being, you have freedom to create
your world. Controlling the senses is your birthright.
Therefore, practice pratyahara to conserve your energies
and, then, concentrate and focus these energies one-
pointedly.

Six Qualities of Mind that Speed Self-Transformation

I will teach you how to create an environment in which
self-transformation can more easily occur. While you are
controlling the activities of the senses and withdrawing
them from their respective objects, you must adopt a
healthy philosophy of life, which will create a good environment for your self-transformation. There are six qualities that will help accomplish this. They are: *shama*, *dama*,
titiksa, *uparati*, *samadhana*, and *mumuksa*.

Shama is quietude of mind, tranquility, equanimity, and
composure. First, learn to compose yourself. Rather than
expecting the external world to conform to your expectations, learn to expect the unexpected. Regard turmoil as
normal and take worldly blows in stride. Expecting things
to be perfect leads to disappointment. Disappointment
and tranquility cannot coexist.

An average person feels happy in response to happy

events and miserable in the face of sad events. Such a person is tossed by the tides of the external world, and happiness becomes purely accidental. To attain tranquility, you must learn not to be influenced by external circumstances. That is the only way to find the state of stillness within. Once you know how to remain still, you can study both the external and the internal worlds.

The second quality is *dama*—self-restraint, self-control, self-mastery, and control over your senses. The activities of the senses are the first step in forming habit patterns. The conscious mind is connected to the senses. It is through the senses that the conscious mind interacts with the objects of the external world. If the mind is not trained properly, then the senses become the guiding force and the poor mind follows them helplessly. This helplessness occurs because the mind gives too much importance to sensory objects and too much authority to the senses. Consequently, they take over.

The senses are like horses. The body is the chariot; the mind is the reins; and the intellect is the driver. The soul dwells in the body-mind organism. If the horses are untrained and are not properly connected to the reins, they can destroy both the chariot and the driver. Even if the reins are strong and held tightly in the hands of the driver, wild horses can still create serious problems.

Therefore, training the senses is of the utmost importance. This training must be based on proper understanding because if you try to restrain your senses without it, repression and suppression will result. Therefore, you must be fully convinced of the importance of being happy and healthy, and understand that control over your senses maintains that state. Using knowledge as the basis for controlling the senses is discipline. Discipline must be lovingly accepted by your mind, not imposed on it.

The third attribute is *titiksa*—forbearance, tolerance, and endurance at the physical, mental, and verbal levels.

Expand your capacity to face every situation and circumstance that life brings. Coping with the world requires endurance and forbearance. Be ready for anything in life because anything can happen.

The body has enormous capacities—it is simply a matter of unfolding them. Do not allow yourself to become dependent on external objects. It is important to live a comfortable life and to have a regular schedule. But do not let comfort make you lazy, and do not let regularity lapse into rigidity. Maintaining a degree of flexibility is also part of discipline. Learning to endure the discomfort brought about by heat, cold, hunger, thirst, fatigue, and sleepiness is part of the practice of titiksa. Develop the ability to adjust yourself to every situation.

Uparati means desisting from sensual pleasure. There is a difference between craving objects and needing objects. You must make a sincere effort to earn your livelihood. After you have earned it, enjoy it. Although you must have means and resources, you should be able to withdraw yourself whenever you wish. You can do this only when you are not involved with the objects you have acquired. If you get involved, if you start analyzing how much time and energy you put into gaining these objects, how hard you worked, how many years it took, and therefore, how valuable these objects are, then you create a strong attachment to them. We bind ourselves with the objects of the world by keeping track of all these details.

If you take your success too seriously, you get entangled and fail to use the objects of your success as a means for the next level of achievement—the spiritual. Thus, right from the beginning of your worldly endeavors, desist from the cravings of the senses and maintain an awareness that although the worldly objects provide some degree of comfort, ultimately, they are worthless.

Therefore, Rama, work hard, but once the work is done, forget it. Think and feel as though you have done nothing. Cultivate an attitude of forgetfulness. Perform your actions, but when you receive the fruit, take it as a gift from above. This is uparati, and it is the ground on which you practice non-attachment.

The fifth attribute is *samadhana*, putting together or arranging in proper order. It refers to putting the statements of different teachers and scriptures in their proper context. There are many philosophies, many instructions and, in most cases, they appear contradictory. For example, it is said that the objects of the world are completely illusory. Like objects in a dream, they are totally worthless. But it is also said that all the objects in the world evolve from God and are meant for God. Enjoy the objects of the world without getting attached to them. If you do not develop the ability to place these statements in proper context, you will be confused.

Another example: It is said that the path of *karma* is as valid as the path of knowledge. Yet it is also said that one cannot attain the highest realization by performing one's actions because it is through knowledge, not karma, that one gains liberation. Without the ability to place these statements in proper context, you will become confused and may wonder, "If actions cannot help me attain freedom, no matter how beautifully and skillfully I perform them, then why should I bother performing actions?" Learned teachers resolve this conflict by pointing out that if you do not perform your actions skillfully, they will create obstacles, no matter what spiritual path you are treading. Performing your actions skillfully allows you to live in this world happily while minimizing the obstacles. If you have samadhana—the ability to put things in the proper context—you will easily understand that the paths of karma and knowledge are complementary paths.

The sixth quality—*mumuksa*—is the most important. Mumuksa is the desire for liberation. Without mumuksa, spiritual practice turns into a mere art. You'll become an accomplished philosopher who is miserable from carrying the burden of knowledge without the benefit of experience. If you study out of curiosity or for the sake of studying itself, you become a pedant or a logician.

Many people know so much that they lose their faith. They keep studying and finding contradictions. Because they lack mumuksa, they do not understand the principle of samadhana—how to put things in proper order. But once you desire liberation, everything falls into place. You become tongue-tied because everything makes sense. You understand that it doesn't make sense to many people, but you will not waste your time explaining it to them because they don't have the strength of desire necessary to understand. That's why the Upanishads say: "Those who think it is known to them know nothing at all. And those who do not think it is known to them might know it." Once you know, you cannot express it because it is so subtle.

You can answer the questions that grow out of mere curiosity yourself. If you study the nature of your curiosity and the source from which it grows, you will find the answers. But you will find there are certain powerful questions that you cannot answer. They don't allow you to sit peacefully, but drag you from one book to another, from one place to another, from one teacher to another. That is the power of mumuksa—the desire for liberation.

These are the six prerequisites students must cultivate before committing themselves to the practice of any spiritual discipline.

The knowledge that Vashistha imparted to the world is found throughout Vedic, Upanishadic, and Puranic (epic) literature. However, *Yoga Vashistha, Vashistha Samhita,* and the portions of the Vedas said to have come through Vashistha are the main sources of his teaching. In *Yoga Vashistha,* he teaches the practical aspect of yogic disciplines related to body, breath, and mind. This unique encyclopedic text falls between hatha and kundalini yoga. It contains precise techniques of pranayama, concentration, and sense withdrawal. The beauty of *Yoga Vashistha* is that it blends yogic practices with the sublime teachings of vedanta (*jnana yoga*). In the 24,000 verses that comprise this text, Vashistha raises and resolves the issues related to almost every aspect of life. The underlying theme is vairagya, non-attachment, and it is fully balanced with *abhyasa*, the actual yogic practices.

However, the highest level of knowledge imparted by Vashistha was supposedly contained in another text, also called *Vashistha Samhita*, which no longer exists. References to this text are found throughout spiritual literature and, based on those references, it is assumed that it was one of the most authoritative texts of the highest branch of tantra, the *samaya* school of *shrividya*. This school is the inner essence of the Vedic tradition, where an aspirant learns the pure yogic techniques of going inward and attaining the experience of oneness with Shiva and Shakti. Fragments from this text are found in the form of quotations in other texts, but the knowledge Vashistha imparted in *Vashistha Samhita* is preserved intact only in the oral tradition of the Himalayan masters.

4

Dattatreya

Dattatreya is considered to be an incarnation of Brahma, Vishnu, and Shiva. Both his father, Atri, and his mother, Anasuya, were themselves famous sages. Because of his profound wisdom and yogic achievements, Dattatreya is viewed not only as a yogi, but also as an incarnation of God himself.

The places where Dattatreya lived and (as people believe) still lives in subtle form are charged with such spiritual energy that even novice seekers who travel there are affected by it. There are several such places in the hills of Nilachala in eastern India and several more in the Himalayas. The most famous site associated with Dattatreya is Girinar in Gujarat on the west coast of the subcontinent.

The ashram of Dattatreya's parents, known as Ansuya in Chitrakut, is still nestled in the beautiful Vindhya Range of the central Indian mountains. A steep mountain towers over the back of the ashram, and the serene streams of the Mandakini River issue from a nearby cave. In the air is a pervasive sense of fearlessness and tranquility.

The fish leap from the water to take puffed rice from the hands of pilgrims. Monkeys come from the forest, greet visitors, and share their food like old friends. Your intellect may insist that they do it out of habit or to get food. But listen to nature and you will hear a silent voice: "Do not pollute the spirit cultivated by sages with your cold intellectualism."

When Dattatreya was still a child, a king visited the ashram. Because his parents were away, Dattatreya greeted the guest. As Dattatreya was making arrangements for the visitor's comfort, the king saw an inner joy radiating from the boy's countenance. Realizing that this was a spontaneous expression of the intrinsic beauty of the boy's soul, the king began to suspect that the boy was gifted with great wisdom. Determined to discover how someone so young could be so wise, the king questioned the child, and the following dialogue ensued.

King: You have been studying with your parents?

Dattatreya: There is much to learn from everyone and everything, not only from my parents.

King: Then you have a teacher? Who is it?

Dattatreya: I have 24 gurus.

King: Twenty-four gurus at such a tender age? Who are they?

Dattatreya: Mother earth is my first guru. She taught me to hold those who trample me, scratch me, and hurt me lovingly in my heart, just as she does. She taught me to give them my best, remembering that their acts are normal and natural from their standpoint.

King: Who is your second guru?

Dattatreya: Water. It is a force that contains life and purity. It cleanses whatever it touches and provides life to whomever drinks it. Water flows unceasingly. If it stops, it becomes stagnant. Keep moving, keep moving is the lesson I learned from water.

King: Your third guru?

Dattatreya: Fire. It burns everything, transforming it into flame. By consuming dead logs, it produces warmth and light. Thus, I learn how to absorb everything that life brings and how to turn it into flame. This flame enlightens my life and, in that light, others can walk safely.

King: Who is your fourth guru, sir?

Dattatreya: Wind is my fourth guru. The wind moves unceasingly, touching flowers and thorns alike, but never attaches itself to the objects it touches. Like the wind, I learned not to prefer flowers over thorns, or friends over foes. Like the wind, my goal is to provide freshness to all without becoming attached.

King: The fifth guru, sir?

Dattatreya: This all-pervading and all-embracing space is my fifth guru. Space has room for the sun, moon, and stars and, yet, it remains untouched and unconfined. I, too, must have room for all the diversities, and still remain unaffected by what I contain. All visible and invisible objects may have their rightful place within me, but they have no power to confine my consciousness.

King: Who is your sixth guru, sir?

Dattatreya: The moon. The moon waxes and wanes and yet never loses its essence, totality, or shape. From watching the moon, I learned that waxing and waning—rising and falling, pleasure and pain, loss and gain—are simply phases of life. While passing through these phases, I never lose awareness of my true Self.

King: Who is your seventh guru?

Dattatreya: The sun is my seventh guru. With its bright rays, the sun draws water from everything, transforms it into clouds, and then distributes it as rain without favor. Rain falls on forests, mountains, valleys, deserts, oceans, and cities. Like the sun, I learned how to gather knowledge from all sources, transform that knowledge into practical wisdom, and share it with all without preferring some recipients and excluding others.

King: And your eighth guru?

Dattatreya: My eighth guru is a flock of pigeons. One pigeon fell into a hunter's net and cried in despair. Other pigeons tried to rescue it and got caught, too. From these pigeons, I learned that even a positive reaction, if it springs from attachment and emotion, can entangle and ensnare. I must give a second thought to my emotional responses, especially if they are related to protecting my own "group."

King: Your ninth guru, sir?

Dattatreya: My ninth guru is the python who catches and eats its prey, and then doesn't hunt again for a long time. It taught me that once my need has been met, I must be satisfied and not make myself miserable running after the objects of my desire.

King: Who is your tenth guru?

Dattatreya: The ocean, which is the abode of the waters. It receives and assimilates water from all the rivers in the world and never overflows its boundaries. It taught me that no matter what experiences I go through in life, no matter how many kicks and blows I receive, I must maintain my discipline.

King: Who is your eleventh guru, oh wise one?

Dattatreya: The moth is my eleventh guru. Drawn by light, it flies from its dwelling to sacrifice itself in the flame. It taught me that once I see the dawn, I must overcome my fear, soar at full speed, and plunge into the flame of knowledge to be consumed and transformed.

King: The twelfth?

Dattatreya: My twelfth guru is a bumblebee who takes only the tiniest drops of nectar from the flowers. Before accepting even that much, it hums and hovers and dances, creating an atmosphere of joy around the flower. It not only sings the song of cheerfulness; it also gives more to the flowers than it takes. It pollinates the plants and helps them prosper by flying from one flower to another. I learned from the bumblebee that I should take only a little from nature and that I should do so cheerfully, enriching the source from which I receive sustenance.

King: Your thirteenth guru?

Dattatreya: My thirteenth guru is the honeybee who collects more nectar than it needs. It gathers nectar from different sources, swallows it, transforms it into honey, and brings it to the hive. It consumes only a bit of what it gathers, sharing the rest with others. Thus, I should gather wisdom from the teachers of all disciplines and process the knowledge that I gain. I must apply the knowledge that is conducive to my growth, but I must be ready to share everything I know with others.

King: The fourteenth guru, oh wise seeker?

Dattatreya: Once I saw a wild elephant being trapped. A tame female elephant in season was the bait. Sensing her presence, the wild male emerged from its domain and fell into a pit that had been cleverly concealed with branches and heaps of leaves. Once caught, the wild elephant was tamed to be used by others. This elephant is my fourteenth guru because he taught me to be careful with my passions and desires. Worldly charms arouse our sensory impulses and, while chasing after the sense cravings, the mind gets trapped and enslaved, even though it is powerful.

King: Who is your fifteenth guru, sir?

Dattatreya: The deer, with its keen sense of hearing. It listens intently and is wary of all noises, but is lured to its doom by the melody of the deer hunter's flute. Like the deer, we keep our ears alert for every bit of news, rumor, and gossip, and are skeptical about much that we hear. But we become spellbound by certain words, which, due to our desires, attachments, cravings, and *vasanas* (subtle impressions from the past), we delight to hear. This tendency creates misery for ourselves and others.

King: And who is your sixteenth guru?

Dattatreya: The fish who swallows a baited hook and is

caught by the fisherman. This world is like bait. As long as I remember the episode of the fish, I remain free of the hook.

King: Who is your seventeenth guru?

Dattatreya: A prostitute who knows that she doesn't love her customers, nor do they love her. Yet she waits for them and, when they come, enacts the drama of love. She isn't satisfied with the artificial love she gives and receives, nor with the payment she is given. I realized that all humans are like prostitutes and the world, like the customers, is enjoying us. The payment is always inadequate and we feel dissatisfied. Thus, I became determined not to live like a prostitute. Instead, I will live with dignity and self-respect, not expecting this world to give me either material or internal satisfaction, but to find it myself by going within.

King: Who is your eighteenth guru?

Dattatreya: My eighteenth guru is a little bird who was flying with a worm in its beak. Larger birds flew after him and began pecking him. They stopped only when the little bird dropped the worm. Thus, I learned that the secret of survival lies in renunciation, not in possession.

King: Who is your nineteenth guru, sir?

Dattatreya: My nineteenth guru is the baby that cries when it is hungry and stops when it suckles at its mother's breast. When the baby is full, it stops feeding and nothing its mother does can induce it to take more milk. I learned from this baby to demand only what I really need. When it's provided, I must take only what I require and then turn my face away.

King: And your twentieth guru?

Dattatreya: A young woman whom I met when I was begging for alms. She told me to wait while she prepared a meal. Her bracelets jangled as she cooked, so she removed one. But the noise continued, so she took off all her bracelets, one by one, until only one remained. Then there was silence. Thus, I learned that wherever there is a crowd, there is noise, disagreement, and dissension. Peace can be expected only in solitude.

King: And your twenty-first guru?

Dattatreya: A snake who makes no hole for itself, but who rests in holes other creatures have abandoned, or curls up in the hollow of a tree for awhile, and then moves on. From this snake, I learned to adjust myself to my environment and enjoy the resources of nature without encumbering myself with a permanent home. Creatures in nature move constantly, continually abandoning their previous dwellings. Therefore, while floating along the current of nature, I find plenty of places to rest. Once I am rested, I move on.

King: And your twenty-second guru?

Dattatreya: My twenty-second guru is an arrow maker who was so absorbed in shaping his arrowheads that the king and his entire army passed without attracting his attention. Thus I learned from the arrow maker to be absorbed in the task at hand, no matter how big or small. The more one-pointed my focus, the greater my absorption, and the greater my absorption, the more subtle my awareness. The goal is subtle, and can only be grasped by subtle awareness.

King: Your twenty-third guru?

Dattatreya: My twenty-third guru is a little spider who built itself a nice cozy web. When a larger spider chased it, it rushed to take refuge in its web. But it ran so fast that it got entangled and was swallowed by the bigger spider. Thus, I learned that we create webs for ourselves by trying to build a safe haven, and as we race along the threads of these webs, we become entangled and are consumed. There is no safety to be found in the complicated webs of our actions.

King: And who is your twenty-fourth guru?

Dattatreya: My twenty-fourth guru is a worm who was caught by a songbird and placed in its nest. As the bird began singing, the worm became so absorbed in the song that it lost all awareness of its peril. Watching this little creature become absorbed in a song in the face of death reminded me that I, too, must develop the art of listening so that I may become absorbed in the eternal sound, *nada*, that is always within me.

Listening to Dattatreya, the king realized that the wisdom of this sage flowed from his determination to keep the goal of life firmly fixed in his awareness and from his ability to find the teachings everywhere he turned. This particular story is from the *Srimad Bhagavatam*. Dattatreya's teachings are preserved in the vast literature of the Puranas and in the *Datta Samhita, Avadhuta Gita, Dattatreya Upanishad*, and *Advadhuta Upanishad*. Many of these works are available in English.

5

Parashurama

Parashurama is one of the most unusual characters in spiritual lore. His father, Jamadagni, and his mother, Renuka, were both great sages. In early childhood, Parashurama was keenly interested in the martial arts and the science of archery, but was indifferent to philosophy and spiritual practice. Although he was kind-hearted in general, he had no mercy for those who violated certain principles that he held to be sacred and toward such people he showed no forgiveness. He loved his father, his mother, and his guru more than he loved himself or God. He would not tolerate even an imaginary slight to these three people but, outside of that, he had infinite forgiveness, mercy, and compassion for others.

His learned father, Jamadagni, was a famous teacher and chancellor of a large education center. He allowed his son to grow according to his natural inclinations and made arrangements for him to study with masters of martial arts and the science of weaponry. In those days, this science far surpassed anything that we know today. Weapons were wielded mainly through the power of thought or involved the use of sound waves (mantras).

Parashurama was a brilliant pupil. He mastered all weapons of warfare that had ever been invented as well as those—as legend has it—which were yet to be invented. He also mastered all of the martial arts. When he completed his training, his skill as a warrior was unsurpassed.

Parashurama decided to remain celibate for his entire life and dedicate himself to the service of his mother, father, and teachers. His plan was to live in peace, but this was not to be.

Upheaval

As fate would have it, Parashurama's father incurred the enmity of a king. One day, he visited Jamadagni's ashram and education center, accompanied by an enormous retinue. To the king's surprise, he was greeted with royal honors. He didn't understand how Jamadagni could afford such a splendid reception, so he inquired about the source of the ashram's wealth. Parashurama's father replied that his cows were his only wealth. When the king pressed him further, he explained that one of the cows—Kamadhenu—was special. This cow was the only one of its kind in the world.

This aroused the king's curiosity even more, and he asked to see the cow. When Jamadagni had the cow brought before the king, the king demanded that it be handed over to him. The sage refused, saying, "It does not befit you to make such demands. This cow enables me to support myself and to provide for the education of all the students living in the ashram. Furthermore, because you are a king, your actions set an example for others. It is a matter of principle: If someone doesn't want to give his possession to others, he should not be forced to do so. I hope you will honor this basic law."

This reply enraged the king. He was determined to possess the cow, but he recognized that if he openly used force against someone as beloved as Jamadagni, the people would rise up and the ensuing revolt might well cost him his kingdom. So he swallowed his anger and decided to bide his time.

When Parashurama learned about this encounter, he became enraged, as he always did in the face of an insult or threat to those he loved. But as the king had made no move to take the cow or to harm his father, Parashurama was persuaded to leave the king alone. A period of time passed uneventfully. Then one afternoon, when Parashurama had gone to the forest to gather fruits and nuts as was his habit, the king sneaked into the ashram. The only person in sight was Jamadagni who was sitting outside deeply immersed in meditation. Seeing his opportunity, the king cut off the sage's head and fled with the coveted cow.

Parashurama returned to find his mother in shock, weeping beside his father's corpse. Rage and the desire for revenge consumed him instantly. He vowed to his mother, "The land that has absorbed your tears will be drenched with the blood of these arrogant people who are intoxicated with the liquor of power."

With full determination, this matchless warrior single-handedly obliterated the king and his entire army. But this did not quell his anger, and he went on to kill the king's relatives and thousands of subjects. Only those who fled the country survived. Parashurama's fury cooled only when he could no longer find any members or supporters of that royal clan.

Almost immediately, his rage died away and was replaced with remorse over his failure to limit his vengeance to those who were responsible for his father's murder. He went to his guru, Kashyapa, who instructed him to devote his time and energy to spiritual practice. So Parashurama immersed himself in spiritual pursuits, and several years passed peacefully. Then, by chance, he heard that a group of people belonging to the king's clan had fled during the war and were now multiplying and prospering in another region. The memory of his father's murder flooded back, bringing with it a surge of uncontrollable anger, and this invincible warrior slaughtered thousands more people who had the misfortune of being distantly related to the murderous king.

When he had conquered the land to which these people had fled and killed everyone who had any connection with them, Parashurama was again filled with remorse and racked with self-condemnation. He was also faced with the enormous task of restoring law and order and finding a competent person to rule the kingdom he had conquered. When this was done, he returned to his spiritual practice, vowing never to kill again. But word of a pocket of survivors reached him once more and, without thinking, he slaughtered them all. This cycle recurred twenty-one times. At last, a desperate and despairing Parashurama went to his teacher and pleaded for help. Kashyapa advised him to take refuge in Dattatreya.

Initiation and Practice

Burdened with guilt for killing hundreds of thousands of innocent people, and filled with self-loathing over his failure to keep his peaceful resolve, Parashurama set out to find Dattatreya. Throughout his journey, he felt as though he were drowning in waves of frustration, dejection, and hopelessness. But as he entered the hills of Gandhamadana and drew near to the dwelling place of the great sage, Dattatreya, Parashurama felt as though the invisible hands of nature were removing the burden he had been carrying for years. Never since his father's murder had he seen such beauty in the earth, tasted such purity in the water, or smelled such freshness in the air. It seemed as though even the plants and animals were enjoying unimaginable freedom and peace.

Parashurama before meeting the sage Dattatreya

From a distance, Parashurama saw Dattatreya sitting on a boulder surrounded by dogs, jackals, snakes, and birds. The aura around his face was brighter than the sun and more cooling than the moon. It appeared that every aspect of nature was experiencing its existence in him and he in it. With this first glimpse, Parashurama was pulled toward Dattatreya like an iron filing to a magnet. He was released from the limits of time and space, and the next moment found him at the sage's feet.

Parashurama introduced himself and began recounting his misery, but Dattatreya interrupted him: "There is no need of recounting your past deeds, oh, son of Jamadagni and Renuka! The past is dead and you are reborn in the present."

With this consoling remark, Dattatreya placed his hands on Parashurama's head, transforming him instantly. Grief vanished. The violent warrior became a spiritual aspirant; the conqueror of enemies turned into a seeker of divine grace. In the company of this great master, Parashurama found solace of mind. As he lived and served his master, he learned the highest wisdom of *shrividya*, the mystical, scientific path leading to the highest beauty and bliss. After receiving formal initiation, he was instructed to complete a twelve-year practice while living in solitude. Parashurama moved to the Nilachala hills in the land of Assam, where he built his hut and underwent twelve years of *sadhana*.

The Nilachala hills are one of the most beautiful places in eastern India, but heavy rain and lack of efficient transportation prevents casual pilgrims and spiritual seekers from reaching them. No trace of Parashurama's cottage or any other man-made structure remains. But the spring from which he used to get his water bears his name and is still flowing. According to legend, the pool formed by this spring was created by Parashurama. It is known locally as Parashurama Kunda—the pool of Parashurama. Spiritual aspirants and adepts find delight in sipping its water.

Parashurama Questions His Teacher

After living in solitude for twelve years and completing his practice, Parashurama returned to his master to receive further guidance. During his prolonged absence, he had formulated several profound questions: What is the cause of life and life's experiences? Where does life come from and where does it rest after it vanishes? Clearly, everything is unstable and in constant flux. All worldly objects seem confusing and mysterious. Human behavior is like one blind person attempting to follow another. Does anyone ever get what he really wants from his "right" actions? And if the desired result is truly achieved, then why do people aspire for more?"

Parashurama approached his master with these questions and a series of dialogues ensued. These dialogues can be found in the *Jnanakhanda* of *Tripura Rahasya*, of which there are several versions in English. This chapter presents a few of these dialogues in shortened form.

Parashurama: Master, it seems to me that the fruits even of good actions are of little value. Whatever is achieved through action is a burden. The absence of happiness is painful, but happiness is transitory. After pleasure ends, a person experiences even greater pain.

Sir, spiritual practice seems no different than any other action. The end result of all these concentrations and visualizations seems illusory.

Dattatreya: My son, you have attained true *buddhi*, pure intellect. You are a rare and fortunate seeker. A seeker who attains such inspired thought is like a drowning man who catches hold of a boat. Worldly people run after tantalizing objects, missing the highest goal of life. A fortunate seeker is inspired to make earnest inquiries and is open to honest and constructive criticism. Discrimination is the first rung on the ladder of the highest attainment.

The ignorant remain caught in the net of confused

thinking. Without clarity of mind how can they decide what is helpful and what is not? Discrimination comes through the grace of the divine force and when she is appeased, she appears in the human heart in the form of discrimination.

After initiation, you completed your practice faithfully, and, as a result, you are now blessed with discrimination. You will find that you are fearless because fear persists only as long as discrimination has not arisen.

Parashurama: Sir, many people seem good on the surface but are wicked inside. Please tell me how to know if a person is good or bad, wise or wicked.

Dattatreya: Purify and sharpen your intellect and let your discrimination and the voice of your heart help you recognize the wise. Decide whether having faith in a particular person will lead you to the highest goal or not. Neither those who involve themselves completely in dry polemics nor those who do not reason at all can be successful in attaining the goal. A person who employs the force of logic and reasoning in the light of the wisdom presented in genuine scriptures attains the highest truth.

Parashurama: There are innumerable scriptures and, in many cases, they contradict one another. Both teachers and commentators differ even about a single scripture. In addition, a person's own intellectual convictions vary with time. Therefore what should a seeker accept or reject?

Dattatreya: Purify your mind and make it one-pointed so that you can understand the apparent contradictions in various scriptures or in the teachings of the sages. Do not allow anyone's teachings or doctrines to confuse you. Select gems of truth from every possible source and integrate them into your personal philosophy of life. Disregard information that diverts your focus.

You can do this when you know how to compromise between reason and faith. First, abandon polemics and form a habit of relying on constructive reasoning. Constructive reasoning will remove your doubts and will convince you that the practice you have undertaken is genuine and fruitful. Then faith will unfold naturally in your heart. Thereafter, faith and constructive reasoning will support and guide each other.

Thoughtful consideration, enriched with faith and constructive reasoning, is called *vichara*, discrimination. The greatest motivating factor in sadhana is discrimination. Through discrimination an aspirant will certainly find his or her path, and through practice a seeker can tread the path and attain the highest goal.

Parashurama: Sir, you said that discrimination is the first rung on the ladder of the highest attainment. Discrimination comes through the grace of the divine force. Her grace is received through meditation. An aspirant is committed to meditation only if he or she is interested. Interest develops after hearing about the glory and importance of meditation and its result. You said that above all else, the entire process depends on the company of the wise. Would you please elaborate?

Dattatreya: The company of the wise is the major way of attaining the absolute good. Here is a story that illustrates my point.

The Company of the Saints and the Highest Wisdom

Long ago there was a prince named Hemachuda, who married the daughter of a sage. To his dismay, this beautiful young woman, Hemalekha, was not interested in sensual gratification.

When he asked her why, she explained, "The objects that are sources of pleasure cannot be enjoyed forever. No one can have everything he or she desires, and a person who gets only a few of those things is not satisfied. In most cases, pleasure is contaminated by suffering. Further, the concept of pleasure seems to be based on the conditions of the mind and one's way of thinking about worldly objects.

The concept of beauty too is merely the projection of the mind.

"Let us take the example of a beautiful woman. Though the woman is outside, the perceiver brings her image inside and evaluates her beauty. If he decides that she meets his standard of loveliness, he projects his conception of beauty onto her. As he thinks about the attractiveness he has projected onto her, he reinforces the idea and, consequently, there arises a desire to enjoy her as an object. As his senses and mind become excited, he begins to experience pleasure. The cause of that excitement is the sense of beauty in his mind.

"Children who have not yet developed this sense, and yogis who have conquered it, are not aroused even though they see the same woman. Conditioned by cultural, social, and ethnic identifications, most people perceive members of their own group as beautiful. Thus the mundane beauty that is generally associated with pleasure and enjoyment is conventional and resides only in the eyes of the beholder."

The wise princess elaborated further on the worthlessness of worldly objects and the painful nature of sensual pleasure. She was so persuasive that the prince lost his interest in worldly objects. But because his mind had been occupied by worldly objects all of his life, his newfound dispassion left him in a quandary—he could neither completely renounce the material world nor wholeheartedly embrace it. He continued to accept the pleasurable objects that were presented to him because he was still under the influence of subtle cravings, but his enjoyment was undermined by self-condemnation and guilt. Out of habit and hidden desires, he was attracted to sense objects, but the next moment, remembering his wife's words, he was repelled. He was constantly upset and felt as if his entire fortune had been stolen. He became gloomy and despondent.

The princess realized that her husband had the potential for spiritual growth; otherwise a dispassion toward worldly objects and a desire for liberation would not have unfolded in him. So she began to lead him on the spiritual path. The first step was to explain that an untrained mind is the root cause of all miseries. "Mind is like a monkey jumping incessantly," she told him. "In order to comprehend the truth, it is necessary to control the modifications of the mind and make it one-pointed, sharp, and inward. Thoughtful consideration, enriched with faith and constructive reasoning, is vichara. Try to understand the supreme goal with the help of vichara. Then make a sincere effort to achieve that goal.

"One who makes an effort with full confidence, faith, and courage can never fail. If you become skeptical because you have not achieved anything with your previous attempts, you become your own enemy. Therefore, with faith, supported by constructive reasoning, select the means to attain the purpose of life and work on that faithfully. There are several methods of attaining the goal. Select the one that is best suited to you.

"But, my lord, before you search for the means, you must decide what the highest goal is. For me the highest goal is that which, once attained, ends suffering. Breathing exercises, concentration on light, contemplation, prayer, repeating mantras, and many other yogic techniques are described in the scriptures as means to attain the highest good but without the grace of the divine force, they cannot lead to the final goal."

The prince replied, "I have heard about the law of karma. I am convinced that pain and pleasure, loss and gain, and success and failure are results of our previous karmas. Our present life is governed by our past deeds; it is an eternal law. How can God interfere with this law, helping some cross the river of pains and miseries, while letting others reap the fruits of their karmas?"

The princess explained that the law of karma is established by the supreme Lord and applies only to those who are not fully surrendered to the divine force.

"Law and order are created by Him,* maintained by Him, and without His will, there is no way to violate them. Purifying one's mindfield, paying off karmic debts, penetrating the vast domain of *maya*, and ultimately experiencing the highest truth is a long process. In this inner odyssey, there are numberless chances to slip from the path and take detours. Whereas, by walking in the grace of God and surrendering the fruits of every moment, the aspirant realizes the sublime glory of the supreme truth easily and quickly.

"To a self-centered aspirant, She grants the fruits of worship and devotion only after previous karmas are exhausted. But in the case of a truly selfless devotee, She immediately grants the highest reward of Self-realization. She does not wait for that aspirant's previous karmas to be exhausted. Because She is an embodiment of infinite compassion, She abrogates the law of karma and speedily guides the aspirant to the highest attainment. After attaining the highest wisdom, the aspirant's karmic debts are paid. Directed by the supreme, divine force, the Self-realized aspirant may come back to work in the world and honor the law of karma, just to set a good example. In such a devotee's case, the law of karma is not enforced; rather it is welcomed voluntarily."

The learned princess went on to describe the nature of the immanent and transcendent forms of God. Inspired by her, the prince studied with learned masters and gained a clear, intellectual understanding of the truth. With the passage of time, he was initiated by his wife and committed himself to the practice of meditation with complete faith and determination.

---

*In order to convey the idea that Supreme Truth or God is neither male, female, nor neutral, the original text uses the terms, "Him," "Her," and "It" interchangeably.

As a result of his sincere practice, he gradually received the illuminating grace to help his outward-oriented mind turn inward. Now he understood the meaning of inner joy. Compared to that joy worldly pleasures were tasteless. However, at this stage of his spiritual practice, he was unable to live in the inner and outer worlds simultaneously. Nor was he able to find the connection between the spiritual and the external worlds, although he was trying his best.

The Prince Tries Solitude

One day Hemachuda asked his wife to elaborate on what is our true nature. To his disappointment, she simply said, "Whatever you feel to be yours is certainly different from you. Go into solitude, learn to discriminate, and whatever you find to be related to you, distinguish it from your Self and thus realize your true Self.

"For example, I am your wife; this automatically implies that I am not you. Renounce everything that is yours. The part of you that cannot be renounced is the Self. That you are."

The prince went into seclusion, sat down, and began thinking one-pointedly, "Who am I? This body is not the Self, because it is born and it changes every day. There are times when I do not experience my body but still remain aware of my existence. Therefore I cannot be my body. Similarly I cannot be my *prana*, senses, mind, or intellect. I do not know who I am and what I am but I feel that I am. I can know things through my mind but how can I know myself? Let me control all my thought constructs. Then I might experience my pure Self."

Having made this resolution, he removed all objects from his mindfield with the skill he had developed in his meditation practice. He was suddenly plunged into a great darkness and was exhilarated because he considered this to be the Self. Curious to know if there was anything beyond this darkness, he controlled his mind, transcended the darkness, and experienced a flash of infinite light. As the light vanished, he wondered what it was. "Am I seeing the Self in all these different forms? Let me control my mind and see what is beyond."

This time he slipped into a deep sleep. Gradually he shifted from deep sleep to the dream state and experienced the projection of his mind. After returning to normal awareness, he began wondering, "Was all of this a dream? Now I am confused as to whether the light and darkness were also phases of a dream. What a tricky mind. Let me try once more."

This time he crossed the stupefied state of his mind and became absorbed in a blissful state of awareness, but eventually his mind slipped back to the ordinary waking state. Then he began wondering, "Was this a mere dream or the experience of truth? It is astonishing. I've never experienced such a profound peace. There is no joy like this. I was not unconscious because I still remember it clearly.

"I cannot explain it. On one hand, I know that I have experienced it, but on the other, it is still a mystery."

The prince returned to his wife, recounted his experiences and asked whether what he had experienced was the Self or something else. The princess replied, "My lord, the effort you made to control the modifications of your mind was helpful. Enlightened masters consider this to be the main means of Self-realization. However, only the knowledge of the Self can be attained; the Self cannot be attained. You can only acquire what you do not already have. Consider this example: An object is shrouded in darkness. When the darkness is removed by the light of a lamp, that object is revealed. Turning on the light to remove the darkness does not create the object. That is also the case with the Self.

"Suppose a man hides a piece of gold and then forgets

where he hid it. When he stops thinking about anything else and concentrates only on the gold, he will find it. He is able to concentrate on the gold because he knows what it looks like.

"In the case of the Self, however, it is more frustrating because people have completely forgotten its nature. That is why after removing some of the thought constructs, they believe they have seen the Self. An unfamiliar image suddenly arises and the aspirant thinks, 'This is *Atman*.' That is why the aspirant must get some concept of the Atman through the revealed scriptures or from the enlightened sages, so that during meditation he or she doesn't mistake the projection of his or her own mind for the Self. Enrich your understanding of the Self through self-study, discrimination, and contemplation. For direct realization, however, keep practicing."

So the prince undertook an intense practice and finally became established in a blissful state. The princess saw that her husband was established in supreme consciousness and for some time she did not disturb him. Now the prince was no longer driven outward by his senses and mind, but was drawn inward.

One day, as the princess entered the room, he opened his eyes but closed them again to reenter that peaceful state. His wife caught hold of his hands and asked, "What do you gain or lose by opening and closing your eyes? Do you not want to share your inner experiences?"

The prince replied, "For the first time in my life I am at peace. Throughout my life, I ran after worldly pleasures, but found no peace. Please be kind to me—leave me alone. Why, after realizing this state, are you still entangled in the world? Why don't you stay in this state forever? Why dissipate yourself in the external world?"

The wise princess answered with a smile, "My love, you have not realized that supreme state of the Self yet. What you think you understand is like no understanding at all. The highest awareness can never be affected by opening or closing your eyes. It is not attained by action or inaction, by going somewhere or staying at home. How can it be supreme if it is attained by closing your eyes and lost by opening them?

"Unless the millions of knots of delusion are loosened, supreme bliss cannot be reached. Failing to recognize the Self or seeing a difference between individuals and God are some of these knots. Untie these knots, transcend the duality of wanting and not wanting, liking and disliking and, finally, let that supreme awareness permeate your waking, dreaming, and deep sleep. There must be no wall between any of the aspects of life. More contemplation, more practice, please."

The poor prince felt deflated but he continued his practice and gradually attained maturity in his realization, becoming firm in that consummate state. After that, he lived as a *jivanmukta* (a soul liberated in this lifetime) while enjoying worldly objects, ruling his subjects, amassing wealth, and administering the kingdom.

Thus Dattatreya demonstrated to Parashurama that the company of the sages is the first step in sadhana and it remains the guiding force throughout. Those who aspire to the ultimate should seek the fellowship of saints. The rest follows naturally and effortlessly.

The Relativity of Time and Space

Parashurama: Gurudeva, in our previous discussion, you explained that there is only one reality, pure consciousness. The objective world, including the mind itself, is mere imagination. While you were explaining this to me, logically it seemed to be correct. Nevertheless, I do not understand why this universe appears to be real. Although many wise people believe it to be unreal, it does in fact exist. Intellectually I understand that the perceptual world is unreal but still I experience it as being real. Kindly tell me why, so my confusion will be removed.

Dattatreya: The cause of this error is ignorance. Everyone has tightly embraced ignorance with their hearts and minds. Through identification with form, this body is perceived as Atman. Similarly, it is due to identification with form that this universe appears to be real. The world appears to a person the way he or she believes it to be. Look at the yogis. Through the practice of concentration and meditation, they experience oneness with their object of concentration. Let me relate a wonderful story to illustrate my point.

Long ago there was a king who decided to perform a grand ritual called *ashvamedha*. According to the rules of this ritual, a horse was allowed to roam freely, closely guarded by the king's army. If the horse entered a neighboring ruler's territory, that ruler must either pay tribute or try to capture the horse.

The king's powerful army easily conquered all the challengers until it came across a secluded hermitage where the arrogant soldiers slighted the resident sage. The sage, who was in *samadhi*, did not get disturbed but his son was incensed, and through his yogic powers he conquered the entire army. The few warriors who managed to escape were astonished to see the young yogi lead the horse and his captives directly into a hillside, walking through the solid rock as if it were air.

The king sent his brother, Mahasena, to appeal to the sage, who ordered his son to release the captives. His son obeyed and the captive soldiers appeared to materialize out of solid rock. Mahasena sent the horse and the soldiers back to his brother. He stayed behind and humbly asked the sage to explain how the horse and the soldiers could live inside a hill.

The sage explained that his son wanted to be a king. "So I instructed him in some specific practices by which he attained the highest yogic power. Through his *samkalpa shakti*, the power of determination, he created a universe inside this hill and in that universe, he rules the earth."

Naturally Mahasena wanted to visit this universe. The sage assented and instructed his son to show Mahasena his kingdom. Using his yogic power the young man pulled Mahasena's subtle body out of his physical body, leaving the physical body in a pit covered with leaves. Then he entered the solid rock, bringing his guest along. Jolted by this separation from his physical body, Mahasena's subtle body lost consciousness, so the young sage united Mahasena's subtle body with a gross body that he materialized in the hill world through his power of determination.

Mahasena regained consciousness to find that the young sage was transporting him across a vast abyss. Above, below, and all around, he saw infinite, bewildering space. He saw remote planets in a pitch black sky. He saw the sun, moon, and the entire galaxy, which seemed to shine like reflections of paradise.

Finally the men landed in the Himalayan peaks and began traveling. Here the young sage was emperor, ruling the earth. Mahasena was amazed by this great yogic power and the world created by it. They spent the day touring the yogi's kingdom and then decided to return to the outside world.

They stepped out of the hill as casually as they had entered. The yogi rendered Mahasena's subtle body unconscious, drew it out of the body he had materialized for him and united it with his original physical body. After returning to his normal state, Mahasena was surprised to see that the world around him appeared to be greatly altered. So he asked, "O great sage, what is this new world you are showing me now?"

The yogi replied, "This is the same country that you left. Several thousand years have passed here, though we passed only a day in the world inside the hill. Here the customs, languages, and land formations have gone through tremendous change. My father is still in samadhi, but, in

your brother's genealogy, several thousands of generations have come and gone. There is a huge forest full of
wild animals where your capital city once was."

Poor Mahasena collapsed in shock, grieving for the loss
of his wife, sons, brother, and nephew.

"Have patience. Is it necessary to grieve for your departed
relatives? Who are the dead for whom you weep? Are you
weeping for the departed souls or for the dead bodies?"
asked the young sage.

Mahasena bowed at the sage's feet and said, "Sir, I am
your disciple. Please help me overcome this grief."

Distinguishing Between the Real and the Unreal

The sage said, "People deluded by the power of maya
do not realize their essential nature and grieve uselessly.
After realizing the Atman, a person overcomes sorrow
just as a dreamer overcomes his or her dream identity and
concerns. After dreamers awaken from a nightmare, they
laugh at themselves for having been anxious. Likewise, a
person who has realized himself and crossed the domain
of illusion laughs at people like you who wail piteously
over imagined losses."

"But comparing the experience of the waking state with
dreams does not seem to be appropriate here," Mahasena
objected. "The objects created in a dream simply appear
and do not serve any purpose. But the objects of the waking state are real and useful. They are tangible, used by all,
and they remain the same throughout the ages."

The young sage replied, "The objects of the waking and
dreaming states are alike. A dream tree serves a purpose
in the dream. Many travelers rest in the shade of a dream
tree and eat its fruit. However, the dream objects disappear when you wake up. Similarly, the things you experience during the waking state disappear when you fall
asleep. A rich person experiences poverty during the dreaming state. Like the objects of dreams, all worldly objects are

constantly going through change. Nothing is stable. The reality of the external world is maintained by your thoughts. If someone thinks this universe is unreal, then for that person it becomes unreal.

"The world you just saw is an example. This whole hill is only one mile around but within it is an entire universe. Was that world a waking reality or was it a dream? Was it real or unreal? One day in that universe is experienced as several thousand years here. Now decide which universe is real. They are like two different dreams—you cannot explain one in terms of the other. You also cannot say that one is real and the other is unreal or that both are real.

"The obvious conclusion is that the whole universe is one's own projection. Without projection, it would disappear in an instant. Stop crying. Consider this world to be a dream. Atman, pure Consciousness, is the canvas on which this universe is painted. Atman is the mirror and the universe is reflected in the mirror."

Mahasena spoke with folded hands, "Sir, through your grace, I am free from grief. However, there is something I do not understand. You said that all this happens through thought but no matter how often I think about something, it doesn't necessarily materialize. Because your willful determination is perfect, you could materialize a whole universe inside a hill. To me, this external world and the world inside the hill coexist. Why then are there differences in time and space between these two worlds?"

The yogi replied, "Willful determination is twofold: perfect and imperfect. Willful determination untouched by doubt is said to be perfect. The absence of doubt is the ability to hold one thought in the mind, excluding all others. This external world is projected through the willful thinking of the creator. Because of this intense affirmation, people believe that the universe is real. You do not have full conviction regarding your own power of will, determination, and projection. Therefore your lack of self-confidence creates an obstacle in materializing an object through sheer will.

"Perfection in willful thinking can be attained through various means such as gems, herbs, yoga, austerities, mantras, and grace. When exercising your power of determination, become so absorbed in it that you are not aware of the fact that you are doing it. Maintain this non-dual state until the intended result appears. In the layman's case, the power of thinking and determination is tainted by doubts and the idea of being unsuccessful. That is what makes one's power of determination and thinking imperfect. The power of determination is veiled by maya. When that veil is lifted, you will realize the perfection of willpower and determination.

"The fact that a thing exists—whether large or small, anywhere or at any time—depends on one's will. I projected only one day in the world I created, but in your universe the creator imagined several thousand years. That is why you experience a discrepancy. In a hill one mile around, I visualized infinity. Therefore you experienced an endless expanse within it.

"Thus you can see that all experiences are both true and untrue. If in your determination, you first imagine a one-mile wide expanse, pairing it with one moment of time, and then imagine infinite time and space, it will appear to you as you have imagined. That is the secret behind the relativity of time and space."

Mind, Meditation, and Self-Mastery

Parashurama: Sir, it seems that this entire mess of seeing and not seeing, knowing and not knowing, and bondage and liberation are ultimately a game of the mind. The way we think or, let us say the way we are determined to think, creates the reality behind our experiences. What is the mind anyway? How is it related to pure consciousness, the Self? Was the mind confused from the very beginning or did the confusion begin somewhere later? Why is one person's mind so clear, positive, and naturally turned inward while another's is not?

Dattatreya: These are the most practical questions you have asked. From a practical standpoint, unveiling the mystery of the mind is more important than attaining the knowledge of the Self, for the Self cannot be recognized if the mind is not properly understood. A properly trained and purified mind becomes a means for Self-realization, whereas a dissipated and confused mind is a source of misery. Let me explain the relationship between the mind and pure consciousness: the Self. Pure consciousness alone exists. However, for the sake of our study of mind and consciousness, I am proposing that mind and consciousness exist side by side.

Consciousness is like an ever-illumined, self-shining gem that is kept in the safe of the mind. The safe has been sealed for a long time. Because of ignorance and carelessness, a thick layer of dust has covered it. The safe of the mind is made from a transparent crystal through which the self-shining gem can radiate, illuminating the safe as well as the area around it. But the dust over the mind created by ignorance is so thick that it is almost impossible to see the gem. More interestingly, it is even more difficult to know about the mind and its functions. Now, in order to find and enjoy that self-shining gem, the aspirant must begin to clean the dust from the outer surface of the mind. First, clean the safe, then try to unlock it. The key is kept inside the safe, next to the gem. This is a paradox.

Before you can get your key from the center of consciousness, you must become familiar with the shape, size, and proper use of the key. For that you need the help of those who have already opened their safes. Such great ones are called realized masters. In their company, you have an opportunity to look at your key, at least from the outside. You can also observe how easily they unlock and lock the safe of the mind, how they dwell in two worlds simultaneously—the external and the internal. This will help you become acquainted with the map for your inner odyssey. Later you will have to make the journey by yourself.

Once the covering dust is removed and the safe of the mind is unlocked, you see nothing but the gem itself. The interior of the mind is ever illumined with the light of pure consciousness. But remember, no matter how securely the gem of consciousness has been locked away, and no matter how thick the veil of impurities, the brilliance of consciousness still flashes forth from time to time. That is why people long for Self-realization. Without exception, everyone wants to attain peace and happiness. Therefore, this gem is never completely forgotten, and the safe of the mind is relatively transparent in places. Perfection can be attained by removing all of the impurities, unveiling the gem, and becoming identical with it.

Parashurama: What are these impurities and how are they created?

Dattatreya: There are numberless impurities; however, they can be put into three major categories: skepticism, karmic impurity, and a false sense of duty.

Skepticism. Skepticism means improper thinking, lack of faith, not believing what is said by scriptures and saints, or not believing in any higher truth. Clearly this is improper, confused thinking. This kind of impurity is associated with those who know little but think they know a lot.

This is the case with many philosophers and learned scholars who know the truth intellectually but do not practice it. There are many reasons why they do not practice but ego and skepticism are the most prominent ones. They may think, "I have studied all the literature of yoga, tantra, vedanta, and so on. I have even done a comparative study of various systems. Therefore, I understand the viewpoints and I know more than all the other great masters.

Since their opinions differed, it indicates that they did not know the truth or knew it only partially. Ultimately, why should I bother to experience any of these philosophies when I have already drawn my own conclusions?"

My son, such people carry the burden of knowledge without any experience just like a camel carries a huge load of salt, not knowing its taste. Lacking in experience, such scholars fight with others, making their own lives and the lives of others miserable. This type of thinking, a great impediment in spiritual practice, is caused by mistrusting or contradicting genuine scriptures. The effect of such confused thinking creates a fresh coating of impurity on the mind, leading the thinkers further away from Self-realization.

In order to wash off this kind of impurity, a sincere seeker must allow the light of the scriptures to penetrate his or her mind and to cultivate faith in the teachings of the selfless, compassionate, enlightened masters. He or she must recognize that disregarding genuine scriptures and masters is an error. The aspirant should have an internal dialogue and convince his or her mind, "At least once in the history of humanity, there must have been one person who was selfless and who knew more than I do. Let me follow that person's guidelines and see whether it helps or not."

Karmic Impurity. Every single action, whether mental, verbal, or physical, has an enormous effect on our lives. The subtle impression of our actions, known as samskaras, are stored in the safe of the mind. Each time we perform an action, we create a little mark in the mindfield. In our numberless lifetimes we have created many such traces, which pollute the transparency of the mind. As a result of these karmic impurities, the mind becomes dull and loses its spontaneous capacity to comprehend the truth about reality, whether external or internal. This karmic impurity also determines the particular species into which a person is born and the length of life in it. A person's inner tendencies, inclinations, and attitudes, largely governed by these impurities, tend to counteract the power of determination. The fewer impurities there are, the clearer a person's mind will be.

The scriptures describe several means of removing these impurities but without God's grace nothing works very efficiently. This is because any method of purification is actually undertaken by the mind. If the mind itself is clouded, then certainly a human being will fail to use the proper methods. However, a sincere aspirant must not be lazy and should continue with the method he has been taught while waiting for God's grace. Through meditation, selfless service, and ultimately God's grace, one attains the goal, whether in this lifetime or in the next, depending on how many of the impurities have been cleared away.

The False Sense of Duty. This third type of impurity is the most difficult of all the impurities to remove. There is no end to worldly duties and obligations. The aspirant must learn to discriminate which are the most important and take care of those first.

Those who are not awakened at all perform their actions driven by their urges and by nature. They remain involved in the world because they do not know other dimensions of life. By the time they complete one project, the next is already waiting. Compared to the highest goal of life, Self-realization, all worldly duties are secondary. As long as this fact is not instilled in the mind, there is no way to attain freedom from worldly obligations.

Without spiritual awareness, turning away from the world becomes a source of misery. Disregarding worldly obligations without any higher purpose kills your conscience. Therefore, instead of working directly to wash off this impurity, simply cultivate dispassion and non-attachment. Through constant contemplation, let the burning desire for liberation grow. Only then will you be able to determine whether to take care of your obligations or to renounce them. You attain freedom by conquering your desires, not by running away from your duties. Remove this desire-born impurity with the help of dispassion or non-attachment. Non-attachment can be cultivated by observing the insignificance of worldly objects. A mind free from desires can easily be purified.

The Purpose of Spiritual Practices

The only purpose of spiritual practices is to remove these threefold impurities. How much practice you need depends on how many of these impurities you have. Commitment to practice comes only with the desire for liberation. Without this desire, direct realization is impossible, no matter how much you listen to a teacher or contemplate a philosophical truth.

Without a sincere desire for liberation, listening, studying, and contemplation are mere arts. Mastering an art does not lead to the highest goal. A weak desire for liberation is useless. A transient desire arising from hearing about the glory of reality is not desire. It is excitement, a momentary curiosity. Such a momentary curiosity is not sufficient to inspire a person to make a sincere effort for attainment. For attainment, one needs *tivra mumuksha*, intense desire for liberation. The stronger the desire for liberation, the more quickly one attains the goal. Intense desire motivates an aspirant to whole-hearted practice. Such motivation and unlimited courage to "carry through" is called absorption in sadhana. Such a desire is sparked when one realizes that everything else is trivial compared to liberation.

Recognizing the worthlessness of worldly objects creates dispassion or non-attachment. The greater the dispassion, the more yearning increases. In turn, dispassion fuels desire for liberation and this desire leads to absorption in practice. Wholeheartedness or absorption in sadhana is the major precipitating factor in the attainment of enlightenment.

Parashurama: Sir, what is this wholeheartedness or absorption in sadhana?

Dattatreya: Resolve with full confidence and determination: "No matter what happens I will accomplish this. This ought to be achieved and I am the one to achieve it." The aspirant endowed with such single-minded resolution overcomes every obstacle. The more a person is absorbed in the practice, the sooner he or she attains the result.

Parashurama: First you said that the company of the saints is the major precipitating factor; then you brought up the idea of the grace of God; and now you speak of dispassion, desire, and wholeheartedness in spiritual practice. Which one is the primary method and how can I develop it? Please be more specific.

Dattatreya: Let me explain the order: the company of the sages, God's grace, dispassion, and absorption in practice.

It is human nature to constantly perform actions, the consequences of which may be good or bad. Behind all action is the desire to attain happiness. Whatever a person's concept of happiness is, he or she makes an effort to attain that. Eventually he or she begins to fear that self-effort may not be enough. At this point the aspirant turns to God, who is said to be almighty and who can fulfill all desires. The aspirant begins reading, questioning whether God exists, asking how to pray, and wondering how much can be expected of God. To find the answers, the aspirant seeks out the company of the wise.

A person may expect his or her good actions to help decrease life's problems and conflicts. But sometimes, his or her charity, austerities, scriptural study, and other good deeds do not seem to bear commensurate fruit. The aspirant also notices that often those who perform good karma suffer throughout life, while evil people are happy. Why?

Unable to answer this question, the aspirant turns for advice to the learned.

Parashurama, when the aspirant listens to the wise extolling the greatness of God and spiritual practice, grace begins to descend; interest in the supra-mundane is quickened; and the seeker begins to tread the path.

An individual must have some good karma from the past for this process even to begin. Coming into the company of a wise person is the most critical juncture in a soul's evolution; it is at this point that his or her true purpose as a human being begins to be fulfilled. The results of meritorious karma lead to *satsanga* (good company), and listening to and associating with those further along the path. The aspirant's interest is kindled and he or she begins to practice.

Through satsanga the aspirant develops faith and learns how to draw the proper meaning from the scriptures. From revealed scripture he or she learns about the absolute reality. If necessary, the aspirant may be taught to conceptualize the absolute through symbols and images. By worshipping the absolute through symbols, the aspirant attains the grace that helps him or her to cultivate disinterest in sensory objects and awakens ardent desire for enlightenment. Burning desire, in turn, helps develop unflagging determination to attain the goal. The aspirant begins listening to the confident inner voice that asserts, "I am going to do it. The goal can be attained and I will attain it."

This is the ground where master and disciple meet. The *sadhaka* surrenders himself to the master with perfect faith. The master teaches the disciple about the non-dual state of reality. At first a student comprehends this only theoretically, believing it rather than knowing it directly. But as he or she applies the method of meditation and contemplation taught by the master, the aspirant realizes the highest truth experientially.

Categories of Enlightened Beings

Parashurama: How does a realized person live in the world and remain unaffected by the bondage of karma if he or she performs actions after enlightenment? Also, please explain why there are differences in the characteristics of the *jnanis* (the knowers of the truth). Do they experience the truth differently, or is there simply a difference in the perfection of their knowledge? Are there various grades of jnanis? If there are, then why? Do they attain different levels of knowledge? Do some jnanis know more than others? Please explain this to me clearly.

Dattatreya: On the basis of the differing levels of their discriminatory ability, the number of remaining impurities, and, most important, the maturity of knowledge they have attained, there are differences among the realized ones, the jnanis. These differences reflect the degree of their perfection of mind, not the incompleteness of their knowledge. The way they behave and the kind of lifestyle they lead is due to their innate characteristics.

Even after attaining enlightenment some innate qualities of the mind persist. The only difference between a realized and an un-realized person is that the knower of truth remains aware of the truth while functioning in the world, whereas an unrealized person forgets the true Self and becomes lost in the world.

After attaining the absolute truth, a person may continue functioning in the world according to his innate characteristics, although inwardly he or she is not influenced by them. An enlightened sage may live in the world just like any other ordinary person, exhibiting his or her usual tendencies while remaining unaffected by them. That is why there are saints and sages with different tastes, behaviors, and missions, though these differences sometimes confuse ordinary people.

A realized being can be light- or dark-skinned; his complexion in no way modifies his divine realization. The qualities of her mind, like the color of her skin, are also the result of the interplay of the *gunas*, nature's intrinsic forces, and they bear no relation to her Self-conscious state. My son, the Self is entirely free from personality. Personality is part of *prakriti* (nature). The jnanis do not identify with nature; hence they remain free from identification with personality traits.

There are three levels of jnanis. The lowest order are those who have glimpsed the ultimate state but are not established there. As long as they are meditating, they may remain absorbed in the supreme consciousness but as soon as the focus of their awareness shifts back into the mindfield, they identify with their limited selves, senses, and body. They slip in and out of reality, going through the pleasant and unpleasant experiences of life.

The second order of jnanis are those who through long and arduous discipline have controlled their minds so well that their minds are fully purified. The yogis belonging to this category are centered in the absolute but their bodies continue to function in the world. To an average person, they might seem "absent-minded"—that is to say that their minds are absent here because they are fully present there. However their stability of mind still requires a conscious effort, practice. They work in the world but never under the pressure of their psychological defense mechanisms or biological instincts. They maintain their physical existence so that they can discharge their previous karmas, which now play themselves out in their natural course. How actively involved they are in the world in their present life depends on how they have decided to work out their karmas. But no matter what, they remain unaffected by life's circumstances.

The highest order of jnanis are completely unaffected by external objects and remain fully established in their true nature without any effort. The intermediate jnanis are "not there, when here," but the highest jnanis can be simultaneously here and there.

These jnanis have attained such a high degree of mastery of their minds that they can focus on several objects at once. To an average person, they might seem scattered. The daily activities of the highest caliber jnanis flow naturally and spontaneously. Things happen by themselves. Their bodies and minds simply get the credit. They make no effort to do anything or to live in a particular way. This is not to say that they live in a vacuum or have no feelings. They experience pleasure and pain and remain aware of good and bad. But they consider these things to be no more than the objects of a dream.

They are like an adult playing with children. As long as they have a body, they know that they are still in the game and therefore act their parts. But they do not set new karmas in motion because they have disengaged themselves internally from the world process. So new desires cannot arise. They are free from liking and disliking, bondage and the concept of liberation; thus they enjoy floating on the current of worldly life. The life of such enlightened sages that we can observe in the world is merely a shadow of their true being. They remain perfectly absorbed in supreme consciousness as they walk, eat, study, or work, finding no difference between samadhi and daily activities. They can engage in several activities at once without slipping from the blissful experience of non-dual samadhi. They are masters of both external and internal worlds. In the drama of life they are both spectator and participant, the master players.

Parashurama: Sir, these qualities of a jnani are so personal, so subtle that they cannot be observed by others. Can you tell me the way to recognize a truly enlightened saint?

Dattatreya: It is extremely difficult to distinguish the enlightened soul from the ordinary man. Only the sage, himself, can describe his inner state or know the depth of his realization. Still a sharp student can instinctively recognize a jnani.

Generally a spiritual person is identified by philosophical insight, selflessness, and a loving attitude. Even an ordinary person can share these qualities to some degree, but they come naturally and spontaneously to the realized being. But remember, my son, the highest jnanis often deliberately hide themselves, for otherwise, worldly people would constantly make demands on them: "Please bless my business," "Grant me a child," "Help me find a husband." Only the most sincere students intuitively recognize an enlightened sage and come to study at his or her feet. Fearlessness, a marked virtue of the true knower, leaves him or her indifferent to name and fame even if he or she decides to undertake a public mission. A realized person may work in the world quietly or openly; either way, such a one remains in divine consciousness, unaffected by praise or blame.

It is hard to describe the exact signs of a realized soul. However the characteristics and qualities described in the scriptures sometimes help a novice seeker to recognize them. For example, the highest knower of truth can answer any spiritual question instantly without relying on books. But a more subtle and definite indication that a person is enlightened is the ability to solve spiritual problems without words. His or her presence, itself, removes doubts and confusion.

Another indication is that sometimes instead of answering a question directly, an enlightened person may lead the student to the very source of the question and let the student find the answer for himself or herself. After the student has found the answer, an enlightened master simply confirms it. However, it is impossible to recognize an enlightened being through these subtle qualities until you have elevated your intuitive awareness to a certain degree.

First apply these standards to yourself. Only after you have measured up to these qualifications are you competent to apply them to others.

These dialogues are a fragment of those recorded by Parashurama's student, Haritayana, in the *Tripura Rahasya*. In addition, other scattered references to teachings occur throughout the spiritual literature of India. However, Parashurama's most systematic and comprehensive instructions on philosophy and sadhana are found in *Parashurama-kapla-sutra*, which he authored himself. This text is one of the most authoritative manuals on *shakti sadhana*, especially that of the shrividya branch of *shaktism*. Although this text is not available in English, an in-depth explanation of it can be found in the book *Hindu Shakta Tantric Literature* by Teun Goudriaan and Sanjukta Gupta.

6

Shankaracharya

Twelve hundred years ago in the village of Kaladi, there lived a learned man, Shiva Guru, and his wife, Araya Amba. Shiva Guru's life was dedicated to the study and teaching of the Vedas and the Upanishads. He was respected throughout the country. Araya Amba worshipped God and served *sadhus*, wandering monks who frequently visited that village.

The couple was childless and as they approached old age, their sadness about this situation increased. One night as they slept, both wife and husband dreamed that the sage, Vyasa, came to them and said, "A great soul has descended. Soon you will be blessed with a son of infinite wisdom and spiritual powers." Shortly after this dream Araya Amba found herself pregnant. In due time she delivered a baby boy, whom the couple named Shankara.

Extraordinary qualities and characteristics manifested in Shankara when he was quite young. He had a sharp intellect and a powerful memory and seemed already to know anything he was taught. By the age of seven he mastered the scriptures, a feat that ordinarily requires more than sixteen years of study.

Shankara enjoyed discussing philosophical principles and spiritual practices with his father, who knew that he would not live long enough to witness the great deeds of his son. One day father and son had a serious discussion regarding the nature of the soul, birth, death, and the process of transmigration. Soon after this discussion Shiva Guru fell ill. As Shankara watched his ailing father getting weaker and paler every day, he wondered how this physical weakness was affecting his father's inner being. What was actually experiencing the pain of sickness and old age—the body, the soul, or something else?

In due time he witnessed his father's death. While other members of the family wept in grief, Shankara was motionless, lost in deep contemplation. People thought that he was in shock because of his father's death and some even thought he had gone insane. He heard and saw nothing. Hours passed. While everyone else was preparing for the funeral, Shankara remained immobile. Suddenly his consciousness shifted, his countenance changed, peace descended, and the knowledge that had been revealed to him flowed into this verse:

> Water rises from the ocean,
> Turns into clouds and rain.
> No matter what shape and color it assumes,
> It flows on, and merges again with the ocean.
> Similarly, descended from the *Atman*,
> This *jiva*, the individual soul,
> Completes its journey and
> Merges again with Atman.

As he sang this verse Shankara raised his hands, elevating the consciousness of all present. His tears of joy washed away the sadness of everyone who had gathered there.

Encounter with a Crocodile

After this incident Shankara lost his taste for worldly objects and pleasures. When life had returned to normal, he asked his mother if he could renounce the world and move on in his spiritual pursuits. Because his mother was old and insecure, she embraced Shankara, crying, "You are my only son. You are the pupils of my eyes. To me, you are the blind man's stick. Don't abandon me, my son. I will not live for a moment without you."

Shankara did not push this matter further but waited for his spiritual mission to take shape of its own accord. One day he escorted his mother to the riverbank. It was a special occasion and the pair joined many other people from the village who were bathing in the river. Suddenly a crocodile appeared, seemingly out of nowhere, and caught Shankara in its jaws. The onlookers shouted, threw stones, and big sticks to frighten the reptile into letting go of his prey but nothing helped—the crocodile began swimming away to the deepest part of the river with its victim. After Shankara had been pulled beneath the surface several times, he called to his mother, "I'm already on the verge of death. If you let me renounce the world, then this crocodile might spare me for the sake of spiritual pursuit."

His mother agreed and began praying, "For your sake, oh Lord, let this crocodile release my son." Instantly the crocodile released the boy and Shankara, only slightly injured, swam happily to shore. He touched his mother's feet and bade her farewell. Caught between joy and sorrow, she watched her son walk away.

Search for the Master

And so Shankara began his journey to find truth. He knew that the intellectual knowledge that comes from reading books and talking to scholars is not enough to unveil this mystery. He was convinced that such knowledge, devoid of direct experience, is like the unprotected flame of an oil lamp sitting under the open sky. Even the tiniest ripple of emotional wind will blow out such a flame. Furthermore, just as a lamp needs oil, wick, and fire, intellectual knowledge requires constant study, logic, and a mentor. And even after the student has studied different texts and teachings, doubts arise that lead to more confusion rather than to a firm knowledge of truth. Shankara did not want to become a mere pedant who spends his life in scholarly debates and finally dies without any inner fulfillment. In order to go beyond intellect, he needed an experienced master.

He traveled far and wide, meeting saints, sages, and yogis, but no one could satisfy him. At last he met the great sage and yogi, Gaudapada. Because Gaudapada was very old and preferred to be left in solitude, he directed Shankara to his disciple, Govindapada who was living in a monastery on the bank of the Narmada River in central India. A long and strenuous journey was required for Shankara to reach the monastery of Govindapada, but when he arrived, guru and disciple recognized each other at once. Almost immediately Shankara received the highest initiation from his master. By the age of twelve, he was recognized as Govindapada's most learned and beloved disciple.

His master knew that Shankara had a mission in life and that when the time came, he must leave the monastery and accomplish the goal for which he was destined. However before sending him on this mission, Govindapada wanted to make sure Shankara was fully prepared and that he had enough inner strength to withstand the blows that often fall on those who live in the world. Govindapada had full confidence in Shankara's intellectual knowledge, oratory ability, and organizational capacities. But he wanted to test the strength of his *samkalpa shakti* (the power of will and determination).

Shankara Commands the River

One day Govindapada called his students together and explained that he was going to undertake a spiritual practice that would last several weeks. He gave strict instructions that no one should disturb him for any reason. To

Shankara he said, "You are in charge of the monastery; unless I call someone or come out, no one should enter the cottage." So saying, the master closed his eyes and went into deep *samadhi*.

It had been raining heavily and a few days after Govindapada entered samadhi, the river rose, flooding the whole area and threatening to sweep the monastery away. At first there was much heated discussion about what to do and, especially, about how to save the master without disturbing him. But one by one, most of the disciples left the monastery, saying that it was Shankara's responsibility to cope with the emergency. Most of them advised Shankara to warn Govindapada or, at least, to transport his body to a safer place.

Shankara remained calm, waiting while the water rose. When the gate of the monastery was being battered by the thrashing flood, Shankara finally spoke: "Control yourself, oh River Narmada. Withdraw yourself lest you shrink to fit into my *kamandalu* (water vessel), where you will remain until my master comes out of samadhi." Thus commanding the river, Shankara placed his water vessel in the center of the gate and, to everyone's surprise, the river receded instantly. When Govindapada resumed his normal state of awareness, he blessed Shankara with the highest gift of grace and wisdom and honored him with the title, *acharya*, which signifies a teacher who is an authority in himself and requires no further support from scriptures regarding what he teaches to others. Thus Shankara came to be known as Shankaracharya.

The Beginning of His Mission

One day Govindapada called Shankaracharya to him, saying, "Your purpose here has been accomplished. Go and share the wealth that you have acquired with the rest of the world. May you be a light to yourself and a light to the world."

Adi Shankaracharya

Shankaracharya asked, "What are your final words for me, Gurudeva? What exactly is the mission you want me to accomplish?"

Govindapada replied, "Be fearless. Let fearlessness radiate from you and dispel the fear in the hearts of others. Neither be a threat to others nor consider anyone to be a threat to you.

"Deliver only the message of the sages that you have received either directly or from the revealed scriptures, such as the Vedas and Upanishads.

"You must neither force nor manipulate others into following you. Rather dedicate your life to the highest truth and let the magnetism of truth itself pull people to you.

"Do not teach principles that you do not practice.

"Do not teach principles that you have found to be true in your direct experience but that are contradicted by revealed scriptures. You must first resolve the contradictions between your direct experience and scriptural revelations. Only then may you teach those principles.

"It's not important to teach all that you know; teach what people need to know and what they deserve to know.

"Guide them so that they improve their lives, become stronger, increase their capacities, gain deeper insight, and progressively become worthy to receive and appreciate higher wisdom.

"Be a *parivrajaka*, a constant traveller. Wherever you go, find out what people are missing and how it can be provided; find a way to interact with people without hurting them.

"From now on this earth is your bed, your arms are your pillow, the sky is the roof under which you sleep, fresh breezes are your fans, the sun and moon are your lamps, and dispassion is your life's companion. Without being burdened by any worldly possessions, be the emperor of the universe. May eternal peace be yours!"

With profound gratitude in his heart, Shankaracharya

placed his head at the feet of his master, received his blessings and left the monastery with a water vessel in his left
hand and a staff in his right.

As this radiant young monk passed through villages and
cities, people from all walks of life flocked to see him. It
was not easy for Shankaracharya to face these crowds: Not
everyone came to learn from him and to share his wisdom.
Many people came to impose their prejudices, superstitions, and dogmas on him.

The 8th century A.D. was one of the darkest ages in Indian
history. There were hundreds of cults and sects, and different groups fought among themselves and attempted to
impose their beliefs on others. The Indian subcontinent
was divided into hundreds of kingdoms and subterritories,
all fighting among themselves. Buddhism had been shaken
to its core by extreme monasticism on one hand and complicated ritualism and black magic on the other. In the
same way, the sublime religion of Jainism was torn between
extreme asceticism and orgiastic tantric practices. Hinduism,
too, was mired in ritualism and excessive priestly practices.

Scholars were busy fighting with one another and defend-
ing their philosophical positions, and the people were confused about what to believe. Kingdoms rose and fell and,
with these changes, power shifted from one religion to another. The adherents of all religions were tired of their
priests selling indulgences and taking advantage of
people's religious sentiments.

Seeing all this, Shankaracharya's heart was moved. The
young renunciate knew that unless people came to understand their true Self, they would not be able to communicate with others. Shankaracharya understood that the
fewer the differences among people in the external world,
the more peaceful the atmosphere would be. Conflict in
either the external or internal world can be overcome only
by realizing the all-pervading, all-embracing absolute truth.
In order to bring about a qualitative change in our indi-

vidual and collective lives, people must build a strong philosophy—one that is practical, functional, and full of life. This philosophy must swallow all differences of creed, caste, and color as well as all other narrow, ethnocentric concerns. People must attain freedom from the guilt that religious leaders deliberately create in the hearts of innocent believers. They must be given a chance to find and follow the path of freedom and independence without leaning on anyone.

As Shankaracharya contemplated on the philosophy and practices of the Upanishadic sages, he realized that the path of *advaita*, the non-dual Brahman, is the only path leading to perfect freedom and peace. With that realization, this wandering prince of renunciation turned back to the external world, dedicating the fruits of his studies and his ascetic practices to his fellow beings who were still involved with the world. Fully determined, he stood as firm as a mountain and delivered his message of non-dualism.

Those with pure hearts and honest minds heard what he said and understood what he meant. They took his teachings into their hearts and were transformed in no time. But the clergy of the different sects and cults were puzzled, as well as deeply disturbed, as they noticed themselves going out of business. One by one, the leaders from all religious groups challenged Shankaracharya but just as the darkness cannot face the rising sun, they could not withstand the wisdom and spiritual power of this enlightened master. Like a powerful sun, Shankaracharya moved from one corner of India to another, dispersing a light so bright that it did not require any proof. Within a year or two, hundreds of scholars, religious dignitaries, and kings became his students.

Without stopping for more than three nights at any one place, Shankaracharya walked all the way from the tip of south India to Kashmir in the north, and from Gujarat on the west coast to Bengal and Puri on the east coast. During this long journey he encountered many scholars, yogis, and genuine seekers, as well as impressive and clever hypocrites. Here are some incidents from this great sage's life which beautifully illustrate the subtleties of his spiritual odyssey.

Shankaracharya's Visit to Benares

Benares has been a center of learning for centuries. People from all over the country long to come and study with the masters of the various arts and sciences who live there. The *pandits* (learned scholars) of Benares do not acknowledge an outsider any more readily today than they did twelve centuries ago. Before the advent of Islam, it had been a standard practice in India to introduce a new system of thought, philosophy, or spirituality by proving its validity in a public debate. The secular rulers did not involve themselves in these debates but others—particularly scholars—could be expected to challenge new ideas and test them rigorously.

Shankaracharya arrived at the holy city of Benares with hundreds of followers trailing after him. One group welcomed him warmly while another group rejected him. A third group remained neutral and waited to see how he would emerge from the scholarly battle that was imminent with the scholars of Benares.

Shankaracharya seemed oblivious to the mixed reactions and to the impending debate. He took a bath in the holy river, Ganga, and informed his followers that he would go to the Vishvanatha Temple and offer his worship to Lord Shiva. This was exciting news because people could not understand how this adherent of non-dual, absolute Brahman could worship God in a temple and yet teach others about the absolute reality without name and form. People flocked to the temple. Many came to participate in the worship; others gathered to see if Shankaracharya would participate in the ritual.

The ritual itself passed without incident: Learned priests recited the Vedic hymns and the devotees, including Shankaracharya, offered the routine ritual paraphernalia. As the ritual ended, Shankaracharya rose with folded hands and spoke:

"Forgive me, oh Lord, for three mistakes: I know and feel that You are all pervading and omnipresent and yet I walked all the way here to worship You within the confines of this temple. I know that there is only one non-dual truth and thus there is no difference between You and me. Yet I worship You as though You are different from me and outside of me. Finally, I know that 'mistake' is simply a self-created concept and yet I'm asking You to forgive me."

It was an astonishing performance—Shankaracharya had managed to offer his worship in an exact, traditional manner without straying from his non-dualistic philosophy. The entire city fell at his feet. Some people were impressed with his intellectual knowledge; others were enchanted with his spiritual wisdom and yogic powers. And some were simply overwhelmed by the fact that he had obtained so much wisdom at such a young age. Shankaracharya found two of his leading disciples—Padma Pada and Totaka—during his stay here.

At the request of the people, Shankaracharya held several discourses at different locations. One of the discourses, delivered under a pippala tree at Jnana Vapi, is particularly memorable. This dialogue provides a glimpse of the traditional controversy regarding the validity of the path of action or the path of knowledge. In the realm of pure intellect, scholars maintain a sharp and uncompromising distinction between these two paths. But in the practical realm, there is a beautiful balance between these two distinct paths. This excerpt from Shankaracharya's discourse at Jnana Vapi shows how the renunciates of his order created a bridge between the path of knowledge and the path of action.

The Discourse at Jnana Vapi

"Jnana Vapi" means "well of knowledge." It also refers to an area that lies behind the famous temple of Shiva in Benares. For centuries philosophers, spiritual teachers, and religious leaders from all denominations have gathered there once a year to discuss spiritual matters. While Shankaracharya was in Benares a spiritual conference was arranged to take advantage of his presence. The questions that people asked and the answers that Shankaracharya gave during this special gathering cover a vast range. The following discussion provides a glimpse of the teachings he gave to the people gathered there.

Someone from the audience asked, "According to you, sir, knowledge alone is the liberating force. The individual soul becomes bound to the cycle of birth and death as a result of its actions. Therefore in order to attain liberation, one must stop performing actions. If that is the case, how is a person to survive in the world?"

Shankaracharya replied, "It's true that ultimately knowledge is the only liberating force. However, one cannot disregard one's duties and follow the path of knowledge exclusively. In fact there is no contradiction between the path of knowledge and the path of action. It is simply a matter of emphasizing a particular path at a particular stage of life. As long as one has not understood the nature of this external world, the nature of one's body, breath, mind and soul, and one's relationship with the external world, one must adhere to the path of action.

"While following the path of action, one must keep exploring its strengths and weaknesses. One must also keep in mind the importance of discovering the inner essence of knowledge. The path of knowledge is superior to the path of action only in the sense that it leads directly to Self-realization. But the path of action is in no way inferior to the path of knowledge because it helps lead the aspirant to the path of knowledge.

"No one can survive without performing actions. The body itself cannot be maintained without performing actions. But if a person performs actions without paying attention to the process of action, to the fruits of the action, and to the attitude toward the fruits of action, then it entangles the doer in the snare of birth and death, as well as in the experiences that come between birth and death.

"Therefore, in the process of performing actions, learn how to be skillful. Most of our actions are motivated either by the desire of gaining something or by the fear of ending up with something we do not want. Thus from the beginning, our minds are focused on the fruit. Consequently when the fruit is achieved, we become attached to it. If the fruit is not achieved, we become disappointed and dissatisfied due to intense desire and expectations. In both cases, fear is the inevitable outcome. Either we fear losing the objects that we achieved through our efforts or we fear we will not achieve those objects.

"This fear cripples creativity and destroys peace of mind. If we are successful, we cannot rest because either we want more or we are afraid of losing whatever we have attained so far. An unsuccessful person is tortured by insecurity and fear of the future. Therefore we must learn how to perform actions without getting attached to the fruits."

As Shankaracharya paused, someone from the audience interrupted, "Sir, even the most ignorant person has some idea of why he or she is trying to do something. Before attempting to act on the physical level, a person thinks about what he or she wants to accomplish. As the objective becomes clear, the person decides on what means and resources to use to achieve that goal and, as a result, performs an action.

"Therefore behind any action there is some degree of desire. The stronger the desire, the more energy is devoted to the task. Due to that desire, a person places a value on the goal he or she wants to achieve. Depending on how valuable that goal is, a person decides which other tasks should be postponed or disregarded. Thus I do not understand how one can even begin to perform one's actions without any desire or attachment to the fruits."

Shankaracharya replied, "I did not mean a person should set a task at random and start performing it without having a goal. There are three kinds of action. First, there are compulsory actions that we must perform for the sake of maintaining our existence: eating, bathing, and cleaning our houses and clothes are examples of these actions. They are not binding.

"The second kind of actions are obligatory actions, which we must perform for the sake of maintaining healthy relationships with others. For example people have karmic bonds with their closest relatives. Those karmic bonds can be loosened only by paying off karmic debts toward those who are connected with us. We must discharge obligations to parents, children, spouse, and even our community and society, although we are often tempted to underestimate the importance of these duties. Deep in our hearts, however, we know that the call of these duties cannot be ignored. Ignoring these duties creates conflict within and guilt and self-condemnation result. Avoiding guilt and self-condemnation is reason enough to perform these actions, even if we can find no other motive. These obligatory actions bind only if they are not performed.

"The third category is actions we perform with the intention of achieving specific objects for either temporal or so-called heavenly purposes. This type of action is binding. It is the nature of the human mind not to be satisfied with performing only the first two kinds of actions, because the mind takes them for granted. The sense of purposefulness, satisfaction, and fulfillment comes when we perform actions that are not mandatory. They are a challenge for us.

"In this area we must learn how to perform our actions selflessly, lovingly, and skillfully. By performing our actions selflessly and lovingly, and by surrendering the fruits of these actions to the higher truth, we minimize the effect of previous karmic bonds. Attempting to attain freedom from the bondage of karma by performing karma is just like using one thorn to extract another. Sooner or later one must reach the realm where there is no possibility of thorns. That realm is called the realm of knowledge.

"The realization that the purpose of performing one's karma is to extract the roots of previously performed karmas will provide the strength necessary to perform your actions selflessly and lovingly without getting attached to the fruits. The fruits of any action then become like an extracted thorn. A wise person sees no reason to be attached to the thorn which she just extracted. Extract one thorn with another, and throw them both away. If possible dispose of these thorns in a way that benefits others.

"It is necessary to have the desire to extract the thorn of your previous karmas. This is not an unhealthy desire; it is the motivating force for performing your actions. It is the desire to keep the fruits that is binding."

This short dialogue is an example of the manner in which Shankaracharya shared his knowledge and elevated the consciousness of those who studied and practiced under his guidance while he was in Benares.

Shankaracharya's Visit to the Himalayas

After leaving Benares Shankaracharya, accompanied by his beloved disciples, Padma Pada and Totaka, as well as a large number of students, walked to the Himalayas. He had read and heard about the beautiful and spiritually vibrant Himalayan shrines. According to the scriptures, many great sages in the past had done their practices and established centers of spiritual learning there. However when Shankaracharya arrived in the area where Rishikesh stands today, he was disappointed to find that all that remained were ruins of huts and cottages of the saints and yogis who had lived there long ago. A tribe of people who did not believe in the higher values of life and who opposed the teachings and practices of the sages had taken over the entire region. This tribe's looting and killing had made pilgrimages to the Himalayan shrines dangerous so they were no longer undertaken.

When Shankaracharya arrived with his followers, the tribe prepared to attack them with bows and arrows. But in the face of the power of love and non-violence that spontaneously emanated from this great sage, the warriors dropped their weapons. Although they could not understand the profound teachings of the master, in a matter of a few days their violent energies were transformed and directed into constructive channels. With the help of this tribe, Shankaracharya restored many of the shrines in the foothills of the Himalayas. The most famous among these is Bharat Mandir.

According to the legend, many of the early, great saints of the *dashanami* order came from this tribe. In fact Shankaracharya founded this particular order with the intention of preparing a spiritual community who would channel all its energies into the defense of righteousness. According to the rules laid down by Shankaracharya, initiates of the Dashanami order do not necessarily need to be renunciates and live a monastic life but can live as householders and gradually prepare themselves for renunciation. Even today, people from other orders call initiates of this order Shankaracharya's army.

Shankaracharya left most of his followers in what is now Rishikesh and, accompanied by only a few close disciples, began his journey to the high mountains. After several weeks he reached the famous shrine, Badrinath. He stayed in a cave known today as Vyasa Gupha, "the cave where the ancient sage, Vyasa, lived." During this stay Shankaracharya taught the Upanishads and the *Brahma Sutras* to his students.

One day Shankaracharya decided to cast off his body.

He told his disciples that no one should disturb him, and withdrew. Soon after, a sage arrived and demanded to be taken to Shankaracharya. The students informed him humbly that their master could not be disturbed because he had decided to cast off his body. "I know," the sage replied, "That is why I'm here. I must see him."

When this sage approached, Shankaracharya knew that this unexpected guest must be someone very special. The sage introduced himself as Vyasa, saying, "I have come to stop you from casting off your body."

Shankaracharya replied, "My time is over and therefore, I must not live in this body anymore. Living beyond the assigned time is a violation of the law of nature."

"Do not worry," Vyasa said. "I grant you sixteen more years from my life. You have not yet completed your mission. You must write commentaries on the Upanishads, the *Brahma Sutras,* and the *Bhagavad Gita.* You must prepare your students so that they can continue the wisdom of the lineage. You must establish seats of learning in the four corners of India from where the knowledge of the Upanishads can be disseminated. Only then can you return to your true abode."

Shankaracharya humbly assented and made his plans to return to the world. In the company of his disciples, he began to walk toward the northern plains of India. Before reaching them, he stopped at a place which is now known as Joshi Matha. Here he established his first seat of learning, now popularly known as the northern monastery of Shankaracharya. Under his patronage, learned brahmins from south India settled here. They were assigned the job of meeting both the educational and the spiritual needs of the local people, as well as those of pilgrims from all over the country. For almost 1,200 years at this northern seat, as well as in many of the shrines in the high mountains, these brahmins have been serving as custodians and meeting the spiritual needs of the pilgrims who come from all over the country.

The Encounter with Kumarila

Shankaracharya also established centers in the east and west of India where people could study philosophical texts and be trained in the spiritual disciplines. However establishing an ideal center of learning in the south was more difficult. At this time southern India was a stronghold of a priestly class of brahmins involved in ritualistic practices. In order to make these practices credible they had selected and popularized only those *brahmana* portions of Vedic literature supporting their view. From this, an intricate and logistically sophisticated philosophy, called *mimamsa*, evolved. Mimamsa provides a philosophical ground for Vedic ritualism.

Shankaracharya faced a great challenge. While he was still in north India, in the city at the confluence of the Ganges and Yamuna rivers, known today as Allahabad, he sought out the most respected Mimamsa philosopher of the day, a man named Kumarila. Shankaracharya knew that if this great man could be convinced of the philosophy of advaita (non-dualism) the word would spread and his success would be assured. He then would be able to introduce the wisdom of the sages in the south.

Kumarila holds a significant place in the history of Indian philosophy. About five centuries before he and Shankaracharya were born, Buddhism had become the dominant philosophy and religion in India. It had developed an unmatched system of logic and reasoning and had become the most intellectually convincing path. However Buddhism had strayed from the original canonical texts, and the yogic and spiritual aspects of Buddha's teachings had been virtually replaced by elaborate rituals.

By Kumarila's time, the monastic culture of Buddhism had taken hold of Indian society. Thousands of men and women disregarded their worldly obligations and duties and joined the monastic orders. They lived in monasteries apart from the villages and did not participate in any social or economic activities. However for meals, thousands of monks would come out with their begging bowls and walk door-to-door through the villages and cities asking for alms. This practice had become a burden to householders who had a hard time feeding their own children but were forced to support a large population of monastics. Meanwhile corruption and fornication thrived within the monasteries themselves. As a result, newborn babies were frequently found at the outskirts of villages and cities. Either householders raised these children or they ended up living in the monasteries, further swelling the monastic population.

Society was silently begging for reformation and Kumarila came forward. As a great scholar, orator, and man of repute, he openly confronted these social abuses. However he was powerless against the existing system. On a few occasions, he gave discourses but was attacked by the Buddhists. He lost the debates because he was not as well-trained in logic as his opponents. Finally he decided to study Buddhist philosophy and logic so that he could gain firsthand experience of its strengths and weaknesses.

Kumarila wanted to study at Nalanda, the famous Buddhist university. But to be admitted he had to convert to Buddhism and be ordained as a Buddhist monk. Only then was he allowed to study with the famous teacher, Dharmapala. This turned out to be an ordeal for Kumarila: Every day he experienced the humiliation and pain of working within a system designed to refute and condemn the views of others. As a learned scholar and practitioner of the wisdom of the sages, he had the ability to present a correct and meaningful interpretation of the Upanishads to the teachers and students at the university, but he could not because the views of other philosophies and faiths were censored. Besides, his reason for being at Nalanda was to study the Buddhist system thoroughly, spot its weaknesses, and refute it.

Years passed. One day while he was sitting at the back of the classroom, tears flowed from his eyes as he listened to erroneous interpretations and unreasonable criticism of the Vedas and the Upanishads. The teacher noticed his tears and asked what was wrong. Kumarila humbly replied, "I feel sad for myself and pity for all of you that you do not know the essence of the Vedas and the Upanishads. Yet because of your prejudice, you are condemning the sublime wisdom they contain."

The teacher was enraged. He ordered his students to grab Kumarila, take him to the roof of the seven-story building and throw him off. The students obeyed. As they were about to throw him from the roof, Kumarila raised his hand and said, "If I have sincerely studied and practiced the wisdom of the sages and if my faith is pure, then I will remain unharmed."

They pushed him from the roof and were astonished to see him land, unhurt, except for the loss of one eye. Kumarila was puzzled. He could not understand why the power of his faith had not protected him completely. He went to the man who had taught him the Vedas and the Upanishads and asked why he had lost an eye.

"Because you used the word 'if,' my son," his former teacher replied. On this path there is no room for 'if.' The perfection of the power of will, determination, and faith is compromised if you provide an option for yourself. Deep down in your heart, you created a seed of doubt. It was reflected on your tongue in the word 'if' and the result was partial protection."

After this episode Kumarila wrote his famous work, *Shloka Vartika*, and prepared intellectually and spiritually powerful students, such as Prabhakara and Mandana Mishra. He also defeated his opponents in debates and taught the path of the sages. However because people were not ready for non-dualistic, absolute knowledge, Kumarila advocated the path of rituals. In a sense, his noble work was limited to the field of religion.

When Kumarila reached old age he resolved to purify himself from the guilt he felt cheating his Buddhist teacher. According to his high ideals, there were no sins worse than lying to one's teacher, learning from him, then ultimately denouncing the teacher as well as the teachings. As part of his purification and repentance, he took a bath in the Ganga and made a fire on the bank. He sat in the fire and, with voluntary control and with conscious awareness, gradually left his body as a specially prepared, slow-burning fire consumed him from the lower extremities to the upper regions of his body. This process took days.

As this was happening, Shankaracharya was leaving the Himalayas for the plains of India. On his journey, he heard about Kumarila's decision to leave his body. Shankaracharya hurried to the Ganga to discuss his plan for south India before Kumarila cast off his body. But when Shankaracharya reached him, he found that part of the great man's body had already been consumed by fire and he could hardly speak. The moment Kumarila saw Shankaracharya approaching, he spoke in a low voice, "You arrived late, oh Acharya. Go to my student Mandana, who in knowledge is equal to me. Exchange ideas. If you can convince him of the validity of the philosophy and practices you teach, he will become your disciple. Thereafter he will be instrumental in your mission. May God bless you and help you accomplish the task assigned by the Divine." Thus this great man left his body, and Shankaracharya began his journey to the south.

The Meeting with Mandana Mishra and His Learned Wife

Mandana was a great teacher of the Vedas and the Upanishads and was famous in his own right. His home was like a full-fledged college—hundreds of students studied there under his guidance. The atmosphere he had created on the grounds was itself a means of self-transformation. Even the animals and birds who lived near this creative teacher appeared to be more educated than the average human being.

As legend goes, when Shankaracharya was still a little distance from the village where Mandana lived, he asked directions of some women fetching water at the well. The women looked at one another and said, "You are on the right road. Mandana's village is still a few miles from here. When you reach there, you will not need to ask where he lives."

Shankaracharya realized that there must be something unique about Mandana's village and his home so he humbly asked, "How will I know which home is Mandana's?"

The women replied, "Wherever you find parrots and myna birds discussing and debating whether this world is real or unreal—know that place to be Mandana's home."

Shankaracharya and his companions were eager to hear birds discussing metaphysics. When they arrived, they found the place was even more impressive than the women had led them to expect. From a distance, the travelers heard young students reciting mantras from the Vedas. The air was fragrant, and the sky was filled with trails of smoke rising from the ritual fires. The beauty of the altars was enhanced by streamers of mango leaves and canopies of banana plants. A peaceful energy emanated from *yantras* and *mandalas* made of colored rice and barley flour. Cows greeted them quietly and their excited calves behaved as though they were telling the residents about the newcomers. The parrots and mynas greeted the guests saying, "Welcome to all of you."

Mandana Mishra greeted Shankaracharya respectfully and inquired why he had come. Shankaracharya told him how Kumarila had left his body in the slow fire on the bank of the Ganga. Shankaracharya also expressed his desire to discuss spiritual matters, especially the true intent of the scriptures.

Mandana responded, "I'm a householder. My first duty is to perform the after-death rites for my guru. You are most welcome and I will gladly discuss anything from the scriptures you wish, but you must wait until I have completed the rites."

Shankaracharya agreed to wait and Mandana began his task. Meanwhile news of the coming debate between these two great men spread like wildfire. People flocked to Mandana's village to be present for the historic event. Preparations were made. The audience was ready. All that remained was to find a competent judge to preside over the debate. This was not easy because the judge had to be at least as learned as the two great scholars. The only person who met this criterion was Bharati, the wife of Mandana, and she humbly accepted the task.

Ritual Practices Versus Knowledge

Bharati: In respect to knowing the unknown, in respect to seeing the unseen, and in respect to staying in tune with the law of the divine, what is the highest and most reliable authority?

Mandana: The Vedas.

Shankaracharya: The Vedas.

Bharati: What is the intent of the Vedas?

Mandana: Rituals are the true intent of the Vedas.

Shankaracharya: Knowledge is the true intent of the Vedas.

Bharati: How do you justify your view that rituals are the true intent of the Vedas? How do rituals help one attain the highest goal of life?

Mandana: All the contents of the Vedas revealed in the scriptures can be divided into two major categories. Certain sections of the Vedas describe facts regarding the nature of unmanifest, absolute truth; the nature of the manifest world; the place of human beings in this creation; and the facts related to birth, death, and transmigration. Other sections of the Vedas describe rules and methods for living in the world, how to interact with others, how to perform one's duties, and how to attain the highest goal of life in successive stages.

It is important to know who created this world, how it evolved, what the highest truth is, and what we are. But it is even more important to know how to participate in the process of creation that has been set in motion by the higher forces of nature. It is important to know how to follow the rhythm of nature and thereby, establish harmony between the microcosm and the macrocosm. Rituals as described in the Vedas are the way to participate in the activities of nature and to forge a link between individual and collective consciousness—the microcosm and the macrocosm.

Rituals show us how to enact the process that occurs in nature. There is a constant process of giving and receiving, materializing and dematerializing, gaining and losing, creating and destroying. Vedic rituals are the way to give and receive. By offering material objects into the fire, we witness the process of materializing and dematerializing. By giving an offering at the end of rituals, we familiarize ourselves with the principle of gain and loss. In compliance with Vedic exhortations, at the end of each ceremony the physical structure in which the ceremony was conducted is offered to the fire. This unveils the mystery of creation and destruction.

Shankaracharya: Rituals are like blankets that veil the truth. They are nets to trap our intellect, forcing us to confine our consciousness to the superficial values of the manifest world. The thinking of a person who believes exclusively in ritual practices becomes confined to this little world. Subtle thoughts of the mind and tender feelings of heart become outward-oriented. Such a person begins to believe that everything can be accomplished with the help of rituals.

Because rituals involve material objects and because there is a system as well as a defined goal, a person's expectations grow and become vivid. When someone performs a ritual and the expected results don't occur, as is usually the case, that person becomes disappointed. In order to cope with the disappointment, the person tries to discover the mistake in the ritual. Then the interpreter, who is usually the priest, takes advantage of the subtle tendencies of the mind of the person performing the ritual and puts the entire blame on the performer: "You didn't do it with the right attitude of mind; you did not follow the exhortations correctly; you did not give the appropriate love offering to the officiating priests"; and so on. Such explanations create and perpetuate guilt.

Furthermore as the ancient portions of the revealed scriptures state, the original rituals were a simple means of channeling one's devotion toward the divine. They did not require help from priests and clergy. However due to ignorance, laziness, or the tendency to lean on others, aspirants want their rituals to be done by someone else, namely a priest. In order to display their expertise and impress their clients, priests elaborate the rituals, causing them to become riddled by dogma and superstition.

As such practices continue it becomes a fad to make ritual performances glamorous, and gradually more advanced and elaborate ritualistic practices are introduced. At this stage, these ritualistic practices are no longer a means either of channeling devotional feelings or of fueling spiritual unfoldment. They become social events, a form of entertainment, and a way to display social status. These practices become cultural activities. But even before they degenerate into cultural activities, these ritual practices have little or no spiritual value.

Mandana: If rituals are so meaningless, then why do the Vedas advocate them?

Shankaracharya: The subtle essence of rituals lies in

their symbolic or contemplative meanings. The inner meanings of rituals must be brought closer to one's day-to-day life. In order to assimilate the spiritual value of rituals, a person not only must perform them, but also must live with the message that is conveyed by them. And the messages that rituals convey are non-attachment, selflessness, and the importance of remaining free from identifying oneself with the objects of the world.

Mandana: Do all rituals have symbolic meanings?

Shankaracharya: Yes. Rituals are like maps of spiritual practices. One cannot reach the goal pictured on the map by simply reading the map and drawing it over and over. In the beginning, in order to become familiar with the spiritual map, one may practice rituals but if an aspirant does not know how to internalize the ritual, he or she may become a good cartographer but will not become adept in spiritual experience.

Ritualistic practices are a means of keeping oneself busy in the external world while maintaining relatively less worldly awareness. Rituals also give people an opportunity to interact with one another in a relatively loving environment. However if they come to a ritual with their worldly attitudes and habits, they will fight even at the altar. Therefore inner transformation, which requires knowledge and the direct experience of truth, is the only way to attain the highest good.

This short dialogue between Shankaracharya and Mandana about rituals and knowledge is just a fragment of a debate that continued for days. As the debate progressed, Mandana's attitude toward Shankaracharya changed. He stopped arguing with Shankaracharya for the sake of argument and began to make genuine inquiries because he wanted to learn.

On the seventh day, Bharati declared Shankaracharya the winner of the debate and Mandana surrendered himself at Shankaracharya's feet. But after giving her judgement in Shankaracharya's favor, Bharati spoke, "Yours is only half a victory since I, the wife of Mandana, have not yet been defeated." Thus it became her turn to debate Shankaracharya.

Lower Knowledge and Higher Knowledge

Bharati: What is knowledge? Are there different grades and degrees of knowledge? And what is attained through that knowledge?

Shankaracharya: When knowledge is attained, nothing else remains unattained. Nothing remains unknown. Upon receiving such knowledge an aspirant becomes established in non-dual awareness. This state of knowledge is called Self-realization. In this state, an aspirant knows his or her true Self and the Self of all. By knowing his or her own essence, such an aspirant becomes fearless. When this knowledge dawns all doubt, conflict, and insecurity vanish. Clear understanding and direct realization make a person feel secure. Such an aspirant remains tranquil even in the face of the grimmest disasters.

Bharati: There seems to be no place for worldly knowledge. Are worldly knowledge and absolute knowledge mutually exclusive? Is one completely meaningless in the light of the other?

Shankaracharya: In the scriptures, knowledge of worldly objects is called *apara vidya,* and knowledge of the absolute truth is called *para vidya.* One who has not attained direct experience of the highest truth does not see the connection between lower knowledge and higher knowledge, whereas a person blessed with higher knowledge not only sees this connection but also has a better understanding of worldly existence.

This point can be made clear by an example. While standing in a valley, one cannot see the entire valley and certainly not what lies on the mountain peaks. But the

higher one climbs, the wider one's vision becomes. Consequently, the climber gains a better understanding of the
valley and everything below, as well as everything level
with his or her eyes. The climber who reaches the summit
can see everything and thus, the knowledge of both the
mountain and the valley is included in the knowledge of
the peak.

Bharati: Is it possible to skip lower knowledge and gain
higher knowledge directly?

Shankaracharya: It is possible but extremely difficult.
In an attempt to climb to the summit of the truth, a person has to begin the journey from the point where he or
she is presently standing. If someone is struggling with
day-to-day existence, that person's consciousness is completely occupied by the idea of self-preservation. If a
person's actions are motivated by desire, attachment, fear,
anger, greed, and so on, that person has little chance of
going beyond the mundane. It will be impossible for such
a person to climb to the summit without first meeting and
overcoming worldly challenges.

In order to be practical and systematic, an aspirant must
understand what this external world is; how the objects of
the world relate to him or her; his or her exact place in
this scheme of creation; and his or her place in the family,
society, and culture. This knowledge will make it possible
to live a healthy life and make good use of one's time and
energy. The more an aspirant knows the ways of the world,
the more successful he or she is while living in the world.

During our spiritual endeavors, most of the obstacles
are created either directly by the external world or indi-
rectly by our attitude toward the external world. Aspirants
spend most of their time and energy trying to remove
these obstacles, leaving very little time for actual practice.
Most of these obstacles are directly connected to our expectations about the objects that we gain through our actions or our expectations concerning the people we love

or those who claim to love us. When we know the nature of worldly objects and worldly love, we no longer have these expectations. Therefore neither this world nor our so-called loved ones can disappoint us.

When we are no longer disappointed by anyone or anything, we'll have no complaints. A mind free from all complaints is an abode of peace. A peaceful mind is naturally inclined to turn inward and explore the nature of higher truth. That is why the scriptures say that with the help of lower knowledge, one attains freedom from fear of death, and with the help of higher knowledge, one becomes immortal.

Bharati: What is the difference between attaining freedom from fear of death and gaining immortality?

Shankaracharya: Attaining freedom from fear of death means attaining freedom from the pain caused by fear of all kinds. To an ignorant person, death seems to be the most fearsome phenomenon. Therefore it is the most painful experience. This fear arises from the thought, "I am going to lose everything." Throughout life, a human being works hard and continually identifies with the successes and failures brought about by his or her actions. Ultimately all actions and related successes and failures are centered around oneself. The more concrete is the image of the self as body and ego, the more terrifying is the thought of losing the body. At the moment of death, a person is appalled by the idea of losing everything—including wealth, property, clothes, furniture, and so forth. That is why even a person in severe pain does not want to die.

However a person familiar with the law of nature—including the law of change, death, decay, and destruction—overcomes his or her attachments and false identifications and goes through a smooth transition at the time of death. The smoother the transition, the smoother the entry into the world the next time. The less the attachment to worldly objects, the more freedom one has to leave the body voluntarily.

Everyone dies—both those who try to cling to objects and those who voluntarily leave things behind. The difference is that the first group is forced out, while the second leaves gracefully. The same principle applies at the time of conception. Some are forced to be born and others enter a body willingly. The first group is bound to drown in the cycle of births and deaths, whereas the second group incarnates. For the first group, birth and death are bondage; for the second, they are part of the divine will, the divine game, and the individual simply plays an assigned role.

Freedom from the fear of death does not mean that a fearless person will never die. Rather it means that such a person has raised his or her consciousness to the level where he or she is free to exit from the body and enter a new body at will. Attaining immortality means gaining the knowledge of the immortal Self and allowing one's consciousness to be fully established in that. This knowledge imparts not only freedom from the fear of loss and gain but also that state of infinite bliss.

With the direct experience of eternal bliss, one attains inner fulfillment and no longer craves sense pleasure. Thus he or she no longer has feelings of loneliness and emptiness but enjoys his or her perfection regardless of external circumstances. Such a person becomes master of the mind and senses. For such a person, satisfaction and happiness lies not in worldly objects but in the decision to be satisfied and happy. Such happiness cannot be disturbed as the objects of the world come and go.

The Seed of Bliss and Divine Will

Bharati: Why is there so much attraction to worldly objects and sense pleasures?

Shankaracharya: Due to *vasanas*, which are subtle impressions of past experiences, the mind and the senses tend to seek the same pleasures they found before. Objects in the external world awaken the vasanas hidden deep in the mind field. The mind projects its sense of pleasure upon those objects and allows itself to be distracted by them. Objects by themselves have no power to attract the mind; rather the mind projects attractiveness onto objects and then becomes attracted.

Bharati: How were these vasanas created in the first place? What caused the mind to gain the experience stored in the form of vasanas and consequently, subject itself to this long, almost unending, chain of experiencing pleasure and pain?

Shankaracharya: The mind begins this process under the influence of *avidya*—ignorance—and becomes so enmeshed that it does not know how to free itself.

Bharati: How does the mind come under the influence of avidya in the first place?

Shankaracharya: Avidya is beginningless. Therefore this process is also beginningless.

Bharati: How discouraging! But please explain the relationship between ignorance and Brahman—your non-dual, absolute truth. Is ignorance a complete and independent category of reality? If so, then you must accept that there are two sets of reality—Brahman and ignorance. If ignorance is not an independent category of reality, then it must be dependent or at least secondary to Brahman. This makes Brahman a qualified truth and therefore, compromises its pure absoluteness. If ignorance is not a category of existence at all, then such a nonexistent principle cannot have much influence over anything, including the mind. Clarify your position please.

Shankaracharya: Ignorance as such, does not exist. Therefore it is neither an independent category of reality nor a category dependent on Brahman. It is an illusion. Mistaking one thing for something else, such as a rope for a snake, is an example of ignorance.

Bharati: It seems incomprehensible to me that ignorance, which is completely nonexistent and illusory, can gain so much control over Brahman, the pure truth, that poor Brahman gets caught and becomes subservient to this illusion. In answer to this question you will say, as do all the scriptures, that this is "the greatest mystery," beyond the realm of verbal question and answer. Therefore, I drop this question altogether. But I would like to know what the mind and the senses are searching for in the external world as they go through pleasant and unpleasant experiences.

Shankaracharya: The mind and the senses are searching for joy and bliss, although they are looking in the wrong direction. They mistake mere pleasure for true bliss. As soon as they realize their mistake, they become disappointed by the transitory nature of the sensory pleasure they have just received. But they repeat this process again, hoping the next experience will be more profound and longer-lasting. But again, they are disappointed and frustrated.

Bharati: Why are mind and senses so interested in finding bliss, or even pleasure?

Shankaracharya: Bliss is an intrinsic characteristic of Atman, the soul. In the outward journey of life it has lost— or at least forgotten—its intrinsic characteristic. However without the experience of bliss, a human being feels empty and dissatisfied and searches for it.

Bharati: There is something called bliss, which is intrinsic to one's inner being, and the mind and senses are searching for that? Regardless of whether or not they are searching in the right direction, at least the intention of the mind and the senses are correct. How can you talk about this with such certainty when you have little worldly experience, especially with regard to sex, which is one of the most powerful drives and greatest sources of pleasure?

At this Shankaracharya remained quiet for a moment.

Then he said, "Please give me six months. I will gain direct experience of the world and then come back and talk to you on the basis of that."

Bharati agreed and so, without reaching a conclusion, the assembly was adjourned and Shankaracharya, accompanied by his two students, Padma Pada and Totaka, went to the high mountains. There he made plans to leave his body, enter another body, gain worldly experience, and return to his own body. He instructed Padma Pada and Totaka to preserve his body in the snow until he returned. In the yogic tradition, this particular process is called *parakaya-pravesha*.

Entering the Corpse of a King

While living in his subtle body, Shankaracharya searched for an appropriate body in which to gain worldly experience. Eventually he found a king in Bengal who had just died unexpectedly. The entire court was in mourning and preparations were underway for the funeral. Suddenly a miracle happened. As Shankaracharya's spirit entered the corpse, it appeared that the king came back to life. No one really understood what had happened. People were happy but somewhat confused because the king did not behave in his usual manner. It took awhile for Shankaracharya to orient himself in the king's body and to become familiar with the people and routine around him.

People assumed that the king's coma had somehow affected his memory and his personality. However he gradually assumed all of his former responsibilities. In the king's body, Shankaracharya began gaining first-hand experience in governing and all the other troubles the head of a country goes through. In his private life he adjusted himself to all the pleasures that attend royalty—dance, music, food, women, and other sensory delights. In the beginning he was aware of his true identity and his purpose in entering the king's body, and enacted the drama with full awareness. But he gradually began losing that awareness and rather than remaining a spectator, he began participating. As the sense of "enjoyer" grew, the awareness of "pure witness" began to fade. There came a point when he no longer knew that he was Shankaracharya. He fully identified himself with the king and consequently, was trapped internally as well as externally.

Weeks passed and then months. High in the Himalayas, Padma Pada and Totaka began to wonder why their master was so long in returning. Finally Padma Pada decided to find out. He went into meditation and found Shankaracharya ruling a kingdom and enjoying its pleasures. In his deep samadhi he attempted to communicate with his master, but alas! there was no response. Leaving Shankaracharya's original body in Totaka's custody, Padma Pada went to Bengal to meet his master in person.

Because he was now a king, meeting Shankaracharya was not so easy. But Padma Pada discovered that this king was very fond of poetry and had a great respect for poets. So he introduced himself as an accomplished poet and offered his services to the king. This allowed him to gain access to the court. He expected his master to recognize him instantly and was shocked when the king remained oblivious. What was worse, His Highness did not even understand the profound but veiled remarks that Padma Pada made to reveal his own identity and to remind Shankaracharya that he was not really a king. Padma Pada was forced to be more direct. He began to recite a poem:

What has happened to you, oh cave dweller?
You have forgotten who you are,
From whence you have come,
Why you have come, and
Your destination.
You have identified yourself with this body.
Thus, today you feel you are young or you are old.

Not knowing truly who you are,
You find yourself sometimes happy,
Sometimes miserable.
Losing the awareness of your true identity,
You depend on objects to make you happy.
Your expectations have grown to the point
That in spite of having lost your teeth,
The light of your eyes,
Your power of hearing,
And the hair on your head,
You run after the mirage of sense pleasures.
One by one, senses are saying
"Goodbye" to you,
But cravings persist and you, the victim,
Do not know what to do or where to go.
Oh, master of senses! Master of mind!
Oh, knower of Brahman!
Light of my soul!
Come out of this dream.
Open your eyes.
Recognize yourself
And know who I am.

This poem awakened Shankaracharya from his kingly slumber. He rewarded the poet richly. When Padma Pada had left, the king gave his ministers detailed instructions on managing the kingdom and its wealth. Then, pretending to have a headache, Shankaracharya went to the king's chambers and left the body the same way that he had entered it. He re-entered his original body, joined his students, and returned to south India to continue his discussion with Bharati on the basis of direct experience.

The Habits of the Body and the Habits of the Mind

Bharati: When you entered the body of the king, what did you notice?

Shankaracharya: It was like moving into a new cottage. The body had to be trained and adjusted to the mind and consciousness that had entered it.

Bharati: But how did you gradually lose your true self-identity? Did your mind also adjust to the habits of the king's body?

Shankaracharya: Yes, due to a strong identification with the king's body, the mind became affected by the bodily *samskaras* of the king. The more that identification grew, the more Self-awareness receded. The lesson I learned is that if one does not pay attention, then the body and mind will interact with each other almost blindly, and this interaction will lead an ignorant person into utter confusion.

Shankaracharya went on to explain the nature of desire, attachment, and the process by which the body-mind organism evolves from the most subtle principle known as *kama*, primordial desire. He also explained the divine nature of kama, which is an intrinsic aspect of divine will. It is from this divine will, known as *iccha shakti*, that the power of knowledge and the power of action spontaneously evolve. As the individual soul begins its outward journey, it keeps moving farther away from the divine nature of kama and as it does so, kama turns into worldly desires and cravings. This same principle of kama, if understood properly, can unveil the mystery of creation, maintenance, and destruction and thus can open the door to enlightenment. However if not understood properly, kama can propel a soul into the path of worldly transmigration.

Discussions related to the oneness of the divine force with the absolute truth and its evolution into the power of will, the power of knowledge, and the power of action lead non-dualism in the direction of *Shaktism* and more specifically, to the sublime philosophy and practices of *shrividya*. The tradition does not usually discuss this particular subject, and Shankaracharya does not mention this aspect of his teachings in his commentaries on the Upanishads, the *Brahma Sutras* or the *Bhagavad Gita*. But shrividya is the culmination of the tradition, which has been most profoundly described in the text, *Saundaryalahari* (which means the wave of beauty and bliss.)

Bharati asked many more questions and Shankaracharya answered them to her satisfaction. Finally she also accepted him as her spiritual master. And thus wife and husband were ordained. After the initiation Bharati retained her name, but Mandana Mishra was renamed Sureshawaracharya.

Shankaracharya Visits His Mother

About this time, Shankaracharya heard that his mother had been very sick and might leave her body at any moment. He planned to see her before she died so he began his journey to her home.

It had become a common practice for people to wait to greet him along the road. As he passed through one village, an elderly couple was waiting for him. They had brought their only son, a young man who had never spoken and seemed to be autistic. His parents were worried about how he would be able to survive after their death and had brought him to Shankaracharya in the hope of a cure. As the couple prostrated themselves at his feet, Shankaracharya looked at the son and said, "Have you been giving your parents a hard time? Why don't you communicate with others?"

To everyone's astonishment the young man spoke, "This world is not worth the trouble of communication. No one understands me so I keep quiet."

Shankaracharya then addressed himself to the parents: "He is a wise soul. The time has come to unfold all the potentials he has. He belongs to me. You had the privilege of bringing him into the world. Now withdraw your attachment to this young man. The world is waiting for him."

The parents gratefully complied and he was ordained as a renunciate and given the name Hastamalaka, which means "one who sees the whole truth like a small fruit in the palm."

At last, Shankaracharya arrived at his birthplace to find his mother counting her last breaths. She was delighted to see him and left her body in the presence of her enlightened son. Her death forced Shankara once again to meet a challenge from a society locked into rigid orthodoxy.

According to the customs of the time, once aspirants took a vow of renunciation they were no longer permitted to associate with their relatives. Not only had Shankaracharya visited his mother; he also planned to perform her funeral rites. Orthodox brahmins found this shocking and adamantly opposed Shankaracharya's presence at the funeral. Some of them went so far as to say that because the woman had died in the presence of her son who had renounced the world, both she and her funeral had become inauspicious. Many people condemned her and refused to have anything to do either with her funeral or with Shankaracharya.

Unperturbed by all this commotion, Shankaracharya prepared his mother's funeral pyre and cremated her in front of her house. Afterwards he raised his hands and said, "May it be my curse or my blessing. From this day forward, the community that abandoned me and my mother will cremate their dead in front of their homes. May it be a permanent practice for generations to come." Those who heard him realized that all social and cultural practices are ultimately man-made. If they are accepted rigidly, without room for reformation, society suffocates. Realizing their ignorance, the people asked Shankaracharya to explain why he had violated the rules of renunciation.

Shankaracharya replied, "You do not renounce your family and relatives merely for the sake of renouncing them. Rather you renounce your little world, your family,

to find a bigger world—the whole of humanity and ultimately, absolute truth. You accomplish this grand goal by
renouncing, not your family, but your attachment to your
family. The stronger your attachments to your own family
and relatives, the less open you are to the rest of your fellow beings.

"On the path of renunciation, you are not required to
be ungrateful to those who have helped you. She used to
be my mother. Why then, is it wrong to express my love
and gratitude to her? It is hypocrisy to claim that I have
nothing to do with anyone anymore. The only thing that
matters is love. Love is the greatest law. No other law can
surpass it."

The people of the community became humble and accepted Shankaracharya as their spiritual guide. They followed the rule laid down by him and adopted the practice
of cremating their dead in front of their homes.

The Monasteries

By this time Shankaracharya had established a monastery
in each of the four corners of India and appointed four disciples to head them. One monastery is in south India—either
the monastery at Kanchi or the one at Shringeri (there is
controversy on this point); one is on the west coast at
Dwarika; one is on the east coast at Puri; the fourth one,
in the Himalayas, is now known as Joshi Matha. The heads
of each of these monasteries are given the title of "Shankaracharya."

According to oral tradition Shankaracharya himself
spent most of his time at a fifth monastery, Karvirapitham,
in the Kolhapur region of central India. This information
seems authentic because his master lived on the bank of
the Narmada river in Nasik and therefore, Shankaracharya
would naturally be more attracted to that place than to
any other. Karvirapitham is the center where legend says
he appointed Bharati, who had the privilege of remaining

with Shankaracharya, as his fifth representative. The lineage connected to this particular monastery is called Bharati. According to some sources, it gets this name from its exclusive emphasis on knowledge of Brahman; according to other sources, this tradition is called Bharati after the first successor of Shankaracharya.

"Bharati" literally means "lover of knowledge." Knowledge is the only thing needed to belong to this tradition. In this context, "knowledge" means *mochakam jnanam*—the knowledge that liberates, which is the only true knowledge. In the lineage of the other four monasteries, the eldest disciple of the previous teacher is usually designated as the successor. In the tradition of Bharati however, the direct experience of the wisdom of the sages is the criterion one must meet to be worthy of holding the post.

There have been times in the past when this particular seat of learning remained vacant for decades because no one could meet the requirement. When a competent person is found, he or she is asked to accept the position. Even then the candidate must demonstrate competence by facing the challenges posed by a learned assembly of scholars, saints, and yogis.

A Shankaracharya of this particular monastery must be well-versed in all systems of philosophy; that is, he or she must have direct experience of the truth as described by all philosophies and be capable of teaching and personally guiding aspirants in any path that suits them. The person who holds this post must honor all traditions and be capable of resolving the apparent contradictions between them. He or she must not identify with a particular caste, race, community, or nationality. He or she must be fearless and must not be a source of threat to anyone. Ultimately, only one who has attained perfect freedom is fit to fill this post. (The qualifications and prerequisites for holding the seat at Karvirapitham are described in the text, *Mathamnaya*.)

Unlike all other subtraditions that sprang from Shankaracharya, the adepts of the Bharati subtradition do not confine themselves to the cells of a monastery but travel freely. Most of them prefer to remain unknown to the public, and they never involve themselves in religious matters.

After a long, long gap, this post was filled in the early twentieth century by a great, learned scholar named Dr. Kurtkoti, who was succeeded in 1949 by Swami Rama of the Himalayas, the founder of the Himalayan International Institute. However after several years Swami Rama renounced this position to be with his master in the mountains.

Conclusion

Shankaracharya delivered the message of the sages of the Vedas and the Upanishads. In this message, there is a perfect balance between philosophy and practice. Although he emphasized knowledge, he maintained a harmonious balance of karma (action) and *bhakti* (love and devotion). On one hand, Shankaracharya taught how to go beyond the realm of maya and attain pure knowledge of absolute Brahman. On the other hand, he showed us how to adjust ourselves to the idea of a personal God or a personified God as a stepping stone to the realization of the absolute Brahman that is nameless and formless.

With the passage of time, Shankaracharya's message fell into the hands of scholars, different interpretations arose, and one component of his teachings was emphasized— knowledge alone. This emphasis on knowledge turned into cold intellectualism. After the time of Shankaracharya, India gave rise to many other philosophers and scholars, who either supported Shankaracharya's teachings or introduced a slightly different philosophy along the same lines. In order to distinguish themselves from Shankaracharya's system of philosophy and spirituality, they developed a system of logic to support their views. They also taught only the portions of the Vedas that supported their ideas and used these references, in conjunction with their own commentaries and interpretations, to undermine the authenticity of Shankaracharya's views.

In response to these scholars and philosophers, many of the students belonging to the lineage of Shankaracharya developed a highly sophisticated system of logic and reasoning. And thus in the system of philosophy expounded by Shankaracharya—known as advaita Vedanta—a high degree of scholasticism emerged. From time to time, in response to this scholasticism the learned adepts of Shankaracharya's tradition reintroduce the practical aspects of this non-dual system.

7

Vidyaranya Yati

In the beginning of the 14th century A.D., the great sage Vidyaranya Yati, was born into a learned and prosperous brahmin family in south India. According to the information available in the tradition of Shankaracharya, Vidyaranya received the best education available at that time. He was expert in grammar, medicine, astronomy, mathematics, poetics, political science, and even architecture. In his early adulthood, he and a group of scholars organized, restored, commented on, and translated vedic scriptures.

Vidyaranya Yati was also known as Sayana Acharya and Madhava Acharya. According to most historians, Madhava Acharya was the name he received from his parents and Sayana Acharya was his pen name. According to other sources, Sayana Acharya was his brother, and Vidyaranya came to be known as such after he renounced the world and became a monk in the order of Shankaracharya.

In addition to being a prolific writer on diverse subjects—mainly the Vedas and vedanta—he was also the teacher of two kings, Harihara and Bukka Rai. How great

137

a personality Vidyaranya was can be deduced, not only by studying his works but also by looking at the teachings he imparted to these two brothers.

At that time northwest India was dominated by Muslim rule, and Muslim kings has begun invading south India. It was a period of social, cultural, religious, and spiritual upheaval. Vidyaranya inspired kings Harahara and Bukka to organize their strength to defend righteousness. Under his guidance these two brothers, sons of an ordinary local king, became the powerful rulers of the empire called Bijaya Nagaram. Nowhere in history do we find two kings ruling the same territory peacefully. Yet these brothers, because of the high caliber of spiritual training they received from their master, were able to rule together. That south India surpasses the north in cultural richness can be credited to the influence of Vidyaranya Yati and his two emperor disciples.

From early childhood, Vidyaranya committed himself to study and spiritual disciplines. He assiduously followed the traditions of the *shrotriya brahmin*—those who strictly study and practice the Vedas and the Upanishads. In such families, the study of the Vedas and ascetic practices are passed on from generation to generation. Taking advantage of his family tradition, Vidyaranya undertook the intense practice of the *gayatri* mantra at the age of 11, when he received the sacred ceremonial thread (*yajnopavita*). Meticulously following all the rules, he continued his spiritual practices for several decades, but at age 54, he felt he needed personal guidance from a *sadguru*—a competent teacher. He left his career and wealth and was initiated into the order of Shankaracharya by a great and learned saint, Shankarananda. At this point, he received the name Swami Vidyaranya Yati.

Now Vidyaranya focused all his energy in *shravana* (study), *manana* (contemplation), and *nididhyasana* (the practical application) of the vedantic teachings of the

Upanishads. However he also continued his intense practice of meditation on the gayatri mantra. Just as he had in his early youth and adulthood, Vidyaranya gained great fame and honor as a renunciate. However deep down, he felt empty and lonely. He knew that there is a vast difference between knowing the truth intellectually and experiencing it directly, and he longed for direct experience.

Vidyaranya Finds His Guru

Vidyaranya was believed to have the highest spiritual attainment in the country but he openly acknowledged his dissatisfaction with his lack of spiritual experience. His followers and admirers thought he was being humble but Vidyaranya knew the depth of his own imperfection. He worked hard to deepen his practice; prayers incessantly flowed from his heart but nothing seemed to work. His desire to attain enlightenment was intense. He began wondering whether the problems lay with him or with the practice itself. Utterly dejected, he quietly left the monastery. By this time he was an old man. His body had already become a burden, and his mind was even heavier. During this spiritual crisis, he was unsure of where to go and what to do but one thing was certain. He had no interest in the world anymore. Passing through a cremation ground situated in a remote place, he saw a person who did not look very cultured but seemed to be completely at peace. While Vidyaranya was gathering his impressions, this man walked toward him saying, "May I have the honor to greet you, sir? It will be my delight to have you as my guest, even for a few moments."

"Why not? I have already wasted so many years of my life."

The man exclaimed, "What seems to be the trouble, learned teacher?"

"It doesn't matter. Who are you and what do you do here at the cremation ground? What makes you so peaceful and cheerful despite your not having any of those things that usually make people happy?" asked Vidyaranya.

Suddenly Vidyaranya noticed a magnificent pavilion—unheard of at a cremation ground—and people spreading carpets on a platform. Vidyaranya did not understand what was happening. He couldn't believe his eyes and asked the stranger, "Who are you? Are you a magician? How did you materialize all this?"

The man responded, "I am a resident of the charnel grounds. Destruction is creation for me. Ugliness enhances my internal beauty. I embrace the things that have been discarded by all. All you see here on this charnel ground or anywhere in the world is *lila*, the divine game of the great Lord Bhairava, who simultaneously creates, maintains, and destroys the manifest world. I am That. You are That."

The bewildered Vidyaranya was now cautioned and pleaded, "Forgive me, sir, if due to my ignorance I appeared to be disrespectful. My only question is: What's wrong with me that I have been practicing my best for more than 80 years but so far have gained no direct experience?"

As this exchange was taking place, preparations were being made for Vidyaranya as if he were royalty. However he preferred to remain at the feet of the dweller of the cremation grounds. The man, who was an adept of the mysterious spiritual path called *aghora marga*, responded, "Your previous karmas and *samskaras* have not been fully destroyed. That is why you have not been able to have the fruit of your practice."

Vidyaranya argued, "Why is it taking so much time to overcome my previous karmas? According to the scriptures, the task of overcoming past karma can be accomplished by doing one *maha purascharna* of gayatri mantra. In my life I have done it not just once but several times."

The sage responded, "Because you were born a brahmin in a scholarly and priestly family, you learned this mantra from a book and began practicing it as a custom. Early on, you became a teacher but you yourself never got a chance to be a student. Therefore things are going very slowly for you. However look behind you. . .”

Vidyaranya looked behind him and saw seven piles of fire: The first six had been extinguished, while the seventh in the distance was still burning. He understood that they were not ordinary fires but did not know what they were, so he asked the sage.

He responded, “These represent seven past lives. Karmas corresponding to six lifetimes have been reduced to ashes. But the *gayatri shakti* has not yet consumed all the karma from your hoary past. That is why the seventh pile is still burning. Therefore have patience.”

“How much patience, sir, and for how long? Have pity on me and help me achieve the goal of my life before this body is dropped off.”

“It is not in conformity with the divine will. Don’t push yourself beyond what you can sustain. Do your practice and in the natural course of time, you will attain the final result.”

Vidyaranya realized that he had found his sadguru. Therefore he begged for initiation—not the ordinary initiation but rather *shaktipata*. The sage told him that it was not the right time but Vidyaranya insisted, “Please, please. . .”

The sage finally relented. He recited the gayatri mantra in Vidyaranya’s ears and told him to sit down and repeat it. When Vidyaranya repeated the mantra the first time, the Divine Mother, the Goddess Gayatri, appeared before him in all Her brilliance and glory. At first glance Vidyaranya was overwhelmingly delighted, but the next moment he was enraged. He exploded, “What kind of Mother are you that you ignore your child and come to his rescue only when he is old? You merciless, stone-hearted Mother! May you turn into stone and stay at this cremation ground!”

As he completed his sentence, she turned into a statue. Instantly, poor Vidyaranya realized what a mistake he had made. Crying for mercy, he ran and fell at the feet of the master. The sage lovingly responded, "I told you to have patience and not make undue demands but it's all right. It was destined to happen. Now stay here. Offer your worship to Her and in your remaining life, try to assimilate the mystery that underlies as well as transcends both duality and non-duality."

How long Vidyaranya lived after this experience and where he dropped his body no one knows. However tradition tells us that he lived a long life, one that probably exceeded 100 years. His teachings were an inspiration to many.

Discourses on Truth and Gaining Access to Atma Shakti

The answers to the following questions have been taken from Vidyaranya's writings and provide a glimpse of his teachings.

Seeker: Can truth be known by logic and reasoning or is it known directly through intuitive revelation or through a combination of both?

Vidyaranya: The actual experience of Self comes from "Self-revelation." "Self-revelation" means the truth reveals itself to the knower. Upon receiving this revelation, the knower of the truth becomes a *rishi* (a seer). It is not that the rishi sees the truth but that the truth shows itself to the rishi, thus transforming the blessed aspirant into a "seer." Truth dawns rather than being illuminated by the mind or intellect.

However the study of scriptures helps sharpen the intellect and keeps us from becoming complacent about our present level of understanding. Logic and reasoning are a function of the intellect, which is a fine instrument for gaining secondhand knowledge. You must train your intellect so that you can read and understand the map of spirituality that the sages drew based on their direct experience.

By following these maps, which we call scriptures, you can safely and confidently tread the path and one day reach the goal yourself. Reaching the goal and seeing directly is called revelation. Reasoning can overcome doubt but if not guided properly, that same reasoning can create even more serious doubt and confusion. Therefore let your reasoning be attuned with the revealed scriptures and, whenever you notice a conflict between the two, rely on the scriptures. Even when you resort to scriptures, you need your intellect to penetrate the intent of the scriptures. While the intellect is a fine tool, it needs to be used properly.

Seeker: What do you mean when you say the world is illusory and *Atman*—consciousness—alone is real?

Vidyaranya: The world is illusory in the sense that everything in the external world is constantly changing. Objects of the world are transitory—subject to death, decay, and destruction. However in spite of knowing this, we fail to remember that the objects we presently have in hand are subject to this same law. But all objects suffer the same fate, whether we believe it or not. Lack of this knowledge results in disappointment.

All worldly relationships follow the same law. When you are young, you never think you will become old although you see those around you age. When your own old age approaches, you become disappointed and frustrated. You try to escape this disappointment by using herbs, medicines, cosmetics, or just by keeping yourself busy. But nothing helps. That which you think you are is constantly slipping through your fingers.

In your relationships with other human beings, the situation is even worse. One who seems to love you today doesn't care for you tomorrow. Your children tell you they love you but eventually they marry and devote themselves to their spouses and children. You are left alone with your own false I-am-ness—which is constantly in flux. It is in this sense that the scriptures say the world is illusory. This conclusion, however, is not meant to dishearten you or make you sad. Rather accept it as a fact and overcome your disappointments.

While you are trying to assimilate this knowledge of the illusory nature of worldly objects, contemplate on the truth that is immortal and not subject to death, decay, and destruction. The truth remains unchanged and witnesses all changing states of worldly objects, including your own body and mind. Once you know that eternal truth, life's successes and failures and losses and gains will no longer be disappointing. Instead of seeing destruction beneath this stream of change, you will see "newness"—an entirely different experience than you ever had before. You will appreciate the process of change, for you will understand that without this change, the world would become old, stale, and stagnant—a boring place to live!

Seeker: Once you know this truth directly from within, are you really free from the bondage of birth and death? Do you become immortal, as the scriptures say?

Vidyaranya: Of course, a knower of the eternal Self—Atman—becomes immortal. This immortality does not mean that you will never die. Rather it means that you transcend your attachment to worldly objects, including your own body, and that you will be able to maintain the joy of simply *being*. Death is a habit of the body, which is composed of different elements and so must decompose one day.

While we are alive, we're motivated by our desire to undertake certain actions. In most cases, they are goal-oriented. Attachment to the fruit of an action leads us to disappointment and misery. If we fail to achieve the fruits of our actions, we are depressed. If we succeed, we become attached. This attachment is a source of fear because sooner or later, we lose what we have gained. Either we must leave those objects we worked so hard for or they are destroyed before we depart from here.

Desire itself is never destroyed, however. Insatiable desire forces us to perform our actions, which keep creating misery. To overcome self-created miseries, we keep performing actions we think will liberate us. Many desires for performing actions and receiving the fruits are not fulfilled in this lifetime, and those unfulfilled desires create the psychological conditions for undergoing birth and death.

To free yourself from birth and death, you must cultivate an attitude of non-attachment toward worldly objects. That comes only when you know that there is a higher truth. Only then, you will not be tempted by the charms and temptations of the world. After knowing the higher truth (*para vidya*), lower truth (*apara vidya*) loses its binding power. In the light of higher truth, lower truth becomes illusory. An enlightened person knows that the external world is like the water in a mirage. It is a waste of time to run after such water, which cannot quench your thirst. Ignore such appearances and seek the oasis of peace and happiness—Brahman, the highest truth.

Seeker: After knowing that truth, do you really experience oneness with the universal consciousness?

Vidyaranya: Yes. The knower of Brahman becomes Brahman (*Bramavit Brahmaiva bhavati*). If you know something other than Brahman, you believe in it. For you, that is the only reality. Your concepts of pleasure and pain, loss and gain, and bondage and freedom remain confined to the objects in your field of knowing. In this tiny, illusory world, you fashion your self-image: You find yourself poorer than someone else, richer than someone else, and so forth. Because of your limited vision of the truth, you remain a victim of numberless self-created complexes.

Thus if you identify yourself as a merchant, you derive delight from getting richer than all other merchants, and you conceptualize heaven as a place where you can enjoy those riches you couldn't attain on earth. For those who live in the desert, heaven is filled with oases and hell has no water. Such concepts of heaven and hell and bondage and freedom parallel our self-image, which itself is a reflection of the circumstances of our little world. In this world, we either love our self-image or hate it. Whatever the case, we are afraid of losing it because we believe it is the dearest thing we have. People with superiority or inferiority complexes appreciate or depreciate themselves but in the final analysis, do not want to lose what they are.

Nevertheless as circumstances change, our self-image changes and falls apart, in spite of all our efforts to sustain it. We can't stop this process of change, which makes us insecure and fearful. This process becomes a continuous death that we experience before the actual death of the body. Thus the knower of the lower reality remains in the lower reality.

However the knower of Brahman becomes Brahman. You are whatever you know yourself to be—this is a simple law. The moment you know you are inseparable from universal consciousness, you become that universal consciousness. Your faith in that consciousness will grow and your self-image will be transformed. You will no longer feel better or worse than anyone else. You become free from all complexes for in you, all complexes and diversities find their rightful place. They become an integral part of you. Their diverse and seemingly contradictory appearances beautify your unified awareness. You understand that you are not "part of collective consciousness." Rather you are collective consciousness.

All changes taking place within the realm of consciousness are natural and do not affect the eternity of consciousness. For example: In a forest there are plants, shrubs, vines, animals, insects, rocks, and so forth. If we look at everything that exists in that forest individually, we will not see the forest as such, although we can't deny the existence of the forest. From the standpoint of an individual tree in the forest, the passing of a particular plant or insect may be a very sad thing but from the perspective of the forest, it's all part of the forest's growth. Even if the entire forest were to catch on fire, it would still exist because the potential for regeneration would be there. The forest as such never dies when its individual entities are destroyed.

Once you identify yourself with universal consciousness, you will experience oneness with all and find great delight in witnessing changes taking place in the external world as well as in yourself. Your fear of death, decay, and destruction vanishes. You become fearless. Because of this fearlessness you love all and reject none, for you know that everyone and everything in the universe is simply an elaboration of yourself. In this state of realization, love alone is your spontaneous expression because that has become your nature.

Seeker: If Atman—pure consciousness—is the only eternal reality and is not subject to birth and death or bondage and freedom, then why do we need to do *sadhana*? Who does the practice and who receives its fruit?

Vidyaranya: Atman is pure, enlightened, subject neither to birth nor death and, therefore, does not require freedom from bondage. It is never bound by any law. It is the mind that ignorantly believes itself to be in bondage and strives for liberation. Spiritual practices are meant to liberate the mind, not Atman. Mind, with all its employees, the senses and the body, does the practice and, if it is lucky, gets the reward. Atman, the pure Self, stands still from eternity to eternity and witnesses the play performed by this master magician called "mind."

Once mind creates the concept of bondage and is convinced that it is bound, it cannot rest until it is again convinced that it is totally free. Unfortunately its conviction of bondage is so strong that it must go through an arduous method of untying its restraints. That is called intense sadhana.

Seeker: Why do you need to do any practice? Why not just study, contemplate, and gain the conviction that you are That and then become That?

Vidyaranya: Through the study and contemplation on the truth described in the Upanishads, you transcend false identification with the non-self, which is destroyed by knowledge of your true Self. You experience yourself as a pure, unalloyed, totally independent wave of consciousness. This much you achieve by virtue of your contemplative knowledge. But in what sense are you a perfectly free being? The unlimited grandeur, knowledge, and bliss within can be brought forward only by awakening and unfolding the infinite power of Atman. You awaken it through sadhana.

Think of it as if you were a billionaire who has completely forgotten about the money he had in the bank. If he remembers he is a billionaire, he is no longer a poor fellow! But having access to his account, getting out the money, and spending it the way he wants is an entirely different thing. That you do through sadhana. You won't have the courage to claim your wealth if you don't know it exists. For that purpose, you need strong, convincing knowledge that cannot be contradicted by false arguments.

The experiences the sages recorded in the scriptures confirming the existence of Atman and its infinite power—*atma shakti*—is like a passbook in your hand. Your unshakable conviction, fully supported by reason and logic, is like reading your name on the passbook and realizing the balance. On the ground of this realization grows a desire to find the source of your wealth. Acquainting yourself with the routes to that destination is like learning the proper system of sadhana. Overcoming doubts about the entrances and exits at the crossroad is like seeking direct guidance from a teacher. Finally reaching the source and attaining that which was already yours is called accomplishment—the realization of not only who you are, but how great you are and how infinite.

During his long life Vidyaranya wrote several immortal works, including the *Commentary on the Vedas*; the Vedantic texts, *Panchadashi* and *Jivan-Mukti-Viveka*; and the encyclopedic, tantric text on *shrividya*, *Shrividyarnava*. In these texts, he explains profound philosophical theories and addresses the pressing spiritual and philosophical issues that we face in our day-to-day life.

8

Madhusudana Saraswati

Madhusudana Saraswati, another pioneer in the tradition of Shankaracharya, was born in the beginning of the 16th century A.D. Initially, he rose to fame as a matchless scholar of Indian philosophy, specializing in *advaita vedanta*, the non-dualistic school of the Upanishads. It was a time of rapid and multifaceted scholastic development in India. Scholars were busy writing commentaries and independent treatises in Sanskrit from various philosophical perspectives. Powerful commentators such as Ramanuja, Vallabha, Madhva, and Nimbarka, and a host of their followers, produced a huge body of literature advocating their viewpoints using the Upanishads, the *Brahma Sutras*, and the *Bhagavad Gita* as sources.

Monks and scholars from the tradition of Shankaracharya rushed to defend their non-dualistic viewpoints from these teachers and their disciples. In the process of attempting to establish the superiority of advaita (non-dualism) over all other systems, the adherents of the Shankaracharya tradition turned advaita into a dry intellectual pursuit. In many cases, the practical aspects of advaita were lost and only intellectual gymnastics remained. Thus, advaita failed to illuminate the hearts of spiritual seekers.

Madhusudana belonged to the school of philosophers who used logic and reasoning as a powerful tool and delighted in tearing apart other systems in defense of the non-dualistic viewpoint. Madhusudana's *Advaita Siddhi* is an outstanding example of this kind of philosophical text. It expounds non-dualistic vedanta and emphatically proves the existence of non-dual, absolute truth. In establishing this theory, Madhusudana refutes almost all existing philosophical tenets, reducing them to the point where they appear invalid, illogical, and practically meaningless. In his presentation, Mahasudana leaves no space for any principle other than pure, non-objective knowledge. In this work, intellect is the ground, logic is the force, and comprehension of non-dual truth is the goal.

Deep down however, the author of *Advaita Siddhi* was more of a spiritual seeker than a philosopher. Although an adherent of non-dualistic philosophy, he was an independent thinker and a true lover of knowledge. As he continued to study, teach, and write, he contemplated the truth that he preached and felt that deep down, he was still empty. This recognition led him to recall the memories of his childhood and the pure and simple spiritual practices he was exposed to in those days. He remembered how much he loved Lord Krishna and how sweet it was to see his parents and other family members worshipping the Lord. Now that he was an adult, he noticed many saints who, though not as educated as he, nevertheless, appeared happier and more spiritually evolved.

When he pushed his intellect aside, the devotional part of his being came forward and soon he fell in love with Lord Krishna. However he could not abandon the philosophy of non-dualism, which he continually propagated in public. Thus he began leading a double life: In the presence of his students and followers, he was a staunch, nondualistic philosopher but in his private life, he was a devotee of the Lord. He was busy lecturing and writing on absolute Brahman but in his personal practice, he worshipped Lord Krishna with the intense desire that one day he would have a vision of Him. As time passed, this burning desire for communion led him to cut down on his lecturing and writing and spend more time meditating on the beautiful form of his *ishta devata* (chosen deity), whom he believed to be the highest godhead.

Madhusudana Moves to Brindavan

Years passed. His practice gradually became more intense and finally, he moved to Brindavan, the birthplace of Krishna. There he met the devotees of the Lord, who appeared to be drunk on divine love. He noticed that they smeared themselves with the dust of the land, which long ago had touched the lotus feet of the Lord. He met the lovers of Krishna who like madmen, embraced the plants and shrubs as though they were embracing the Lord incarnate. He tried to create such devotional moods artificially by doing what others did but he couldn't feel the slightest touch of the ecstasy they seemed to be experiencing.

He would approach the devotees of the Lord, prostrate at their feet, beg for their mercy and grace, and seek their blessing so that one day he too could see the Lord. One would tell him, "Rub the dust of this land all over your body and tune your mind and heart to the songs of the birds who are constantly singing the praises of the Lord. Through the specks of dust you will feel His touch. In the songs of the birds you will hear His name."

Madhusudana tried but it didn't work. Others would say, "Go to the River Yamuna and take a dip in the water that resembles the blue complexion of the Lord. Ask the river whether she has seen the Lord recently sporting with

His playmates on her bank. Ask the Kadamba tree whether it has seen the Lord sitting somewhere on its branch. Open your eyes, Oh Madhusudana. This entire land is totally pervaded by the Lord. Purify yourself in the holy land of Brindavan. You will see Him, hear Him, smell Him, and touch Him."

Others would say, "Open your heart and wait for the Lord to come in. Break down the doors made of your intellectual knowledge and you will instantly see that He is more eagerly awaiting you than you are Him."

All this made very little sense to Madhusudana. But one night he dreamed that someone told him to go to the holy city of Benares and attain proper initiation on the path of divine love directly from the master. Only then would he attain a glimpse of the Lord.

A Journey to Benares

In Benares, he met a mysterious saint who was known to few in the city. When this man came forward spontaneously to offer guidance, Madhusudana asked him who he was. He said, "I am Bhairava, the destroyer of the world that stands on the ground of illusion."

A beautifully mysterious and profound dialogue ensued between Madhusudana and this sage. What follows is a fragment from that dialogue.

Madhusudana: Why is it that I am constantly searching for the Lord but so far, He has not given me His *darshana*, a glimpse of His real presence?

Sage: In your case, your philosophy itself is the barrier between you and the Lord. There is a conflict between your philosophy and actual practice. Philosophically you are feeding your intellect with the idea of absolute Brahman, which transcends all names and forms. You tell yourself that absolute truth is without any qualities and characteristics—that it is completely different from this manifest world, as well as any kind of personal God you have conceptualized. This philosophy itself minimizes the impact of your *sadhana*, which inclines you to have a direct experience of a God, who is not transcendent but immanent.

The kind of Lord Krishna that comes to your mind has a form and a name and is endowed with certain qualities and characteristics. He is someone whom you can talk to. He is tangible, perceivable. A God with these qualities contradicts the Brahman of your philosophy. Because you never acknowledged this conflict, you have made your spiritual life a battlefield and you are fighting on both sides. For a few hours a day, you want your Brahman, the absolute reality, to supersede Krishna. And for the next few hours, you want Lord Krishna to play His flute for you. How is it possible? You are in limbo.

Madhusudana: How can I overcome this conflict, Master?

Sage: You are not innocent, Madhusudana, and that's why it's hard for you to overcome it. You are a powerful intellectual but you have nurtured your devotional virtues to a high degree. Regular methods of meditation, contemplation, prayer, and other yogic techniques will not easily allow your devotion to conquer your intellect or vice-versa.

Madhusudana: Am I a hopeless case?

Sage: Not at all. You have already received the grace of the Lord; that's how you got here. You need the final touch and you will be there. Now go to Brindavan and do your sadhana. That land, which the scriptures call Goloka Dhama, is a connecting link between this world and the subtle realm of the Lord. In this eternal world of Goloka Dhama, the Lord sports with His shaktis, and blessed souls enjoy their company and that of the Lord's.

Just as the darkness of the night is dispelled by dawn, the vision of the Lord will dispel your intellectual confusion and emotional instability. You will be free from conflict, and the next moment you will see the rising sun, the Lord in His full brilliance and glory. May that mystery be unveiled to you.

The Vision of the Lord

With his master's blessings and instructions, Madhusudana returned to the land of Brindavan and engaged in
intense sadhana. As he neared the day of enlightenment,
his heart was filled with intense love and longing for the
Lord. His intellect began to lose the power to chase away
the force of his devotion. The *maya* that he previously considered to be negative and binding appeared as the divine
consort of Brahman. The Brahman that previously seemed
inactive, passive, and practically inanimate now appeared
to be vibrant and internally pulsating with intrinsic ripples
of bliss and beauty.

This realization was incomprehensible and yet he felt it.
The paradoxical experience puzzled him. He was overwhelmed. Not knowing what to make of it, he simply surrendered himself to it and prayed to the Lord to give him
strength so that he could understand and appreciate the
experience he was undergoing.

As the moment of the vision approached, he was trans-
ported into a state of trance. In this state, *he was totally one
with the Lord. He was the Lord.* But that's not what he
wanted. He wanted to have a vision of the Lord, and that
was possible only if the Lord was somewhat different from
him. He wanted a taste of the divine love that a devotee
receives from the loving glance of the Lord. Through the
grace of God, he walked back from this state of oneness
and found himself in a state where he and the Lord were
on equal ground. How embarrassed he was to see the
Lord and himself on the same platform! With humility, he
stepped back and saw the Lord on a higher platform.

But it was still an experience in the realm of his inner
awareness. The Lord knew that Madhusudana wanted to
see Him in totally manifest form-not only through the eye
of the mind but also through his physical eyes. Through
the power of grace, Madhusudana's mind, which was still
absorbed within, was now pulled outward. He became

aware of his physical existence. With that awareness, he opened his eyes and saw the Lord standing in front of him. At the vision of the Lord, he once again went into a trance, though he was still awake. Words rushed forward, not from the tongue but rather from the depth of his soul. He knelt with folded hands and prayed:

I see the beautiful flute in Thy hand.
How captivating is the blue aura that emanates from Thy body!
How golden are the clothes You are wearing!
How can I grasp the redness of Thy lips that are so celestially bright?
How illuminating and cooling is Thy countenance, which surpasses the beauty and delight of a million full moons.
The only words I find to describe Thine eyes are that they are like lotus blossoms.
I do not know any higher truth than my Lord Krishna.

Madhusudana's Transformation

How can anyone describe the internal states of Madhusudana upon receiving this vision if he, himself, could not do so? However a tremendous transformation spontaneously followed. This experience enlightened both his mind and heart. Knowledge and devotion manifested in him in their perfect brilliance and glory. The highest degree of intellectual grasp and devotional ecstasy manifested in his thought, speech, and action. Philosophers and spiritual seekers alike sought his guidance. Even those who did not belong to the Shankaracharya order honored his words as final authority.

After attaining the vision of the Lord, Madhusudana clearly saw the shortcomings of scholarly writings, especially those which strictly advocated the path of knowledge. From that time on, Madhusudana claimed that knowledge without *bhakti* is like an ocean that lacks fresh water and thus fails to quench one's thirst. His powerful transformational philosophy and spiritual teachings are clearly reflected in his later writings—for example, *The Commentary on the Bhagavad Gita*. In this text, he leads aspirants away from either extreme—intellectualism or devotionalism—and toward the original approach of the ancient Upanishadic sages, which was more balanced than that of the adherents of the sectarian philosophies and religions of the medieval period.

How God Is Both Immanent and Transcendent

Madhusudana Saraswati's integral approach can be glimpsed in his answers to the questions that follow.

Seeker: How can God, the highest truth, simultaneously be transcendent and immanent and thus, respond to your love and devotion? According to *advaita bhakti*, the non-dualistic path of love and devotion, one can be inseparable from God and at the same time, be different from God. How is this possible?

Madhusudana: The truth is not subject to our belief or disbelief. It remains transcendent even if we believe it to be immanent. However under certain conditions, the transcendental truth is experienced as immanent. Yet its transcendence is ever maintained.

Atman is pure consciousness. It is absolute, transcendent, unchanging, eternal, and always free. However as the stream of life manifests from this source, Atman, it assumes a form. This form consists of multiple layers of reality. Some of these layers are more subtle, invisible, and intangible than others. In these different layers of our being, consciousness flows in various grades and degrees. That is to say, the existence of transcendental Atman is experienced differently at each level.

Based on our self-awareness, we identify ourselves variously from level to level. When we are aware of our bodies, we think ourselves to be bodies; when we are aware of the mind, we think ourselves to be mind, and at the awareness of the individual self, we feel that we are different than the mind but are still separate from other human beings. At each level, we derive different kinds of satisfaction from diverse relationships. The body receives pleasure from a physical relationship, the mind from a psychological relationship, and the individual self from a personal relationship with the higher Self. Atman, however, delights in itself.

For those whose consciousness is confined to the body and the external world, the idea of pure, transcendental truth seems a mere fiction. For them, God must be tangible, localized, and capable of responding to their needs. Although there is no such God, still the transcendental God that is one with the Self seeps through a person's individual self, mind, and brain, and an image of God is sculpted. This God is never more real or unreal than our own bodies. Just as we cannot expect to secure our mental health if we ignore our physical health, we face numberless obstacles on our inward journey if we ignore this personal God. However just as the totality of our existence is not confined only to the body and our peace and happiness is not confined only to physical pleasure, the worship of an external image of God cannot give complete fulfillment.

A sincere seeker can use this kind of God and his or her relationship with Him as a stepping stone to the next level of realization. From that standpoint, it is perfectly correct that God is immanent, and that an individual entirely different from God requires His mercy to overcome the present level of pain and misery that forces the aspirant to remain caught in body consciousness. However the process of God-realization must go to the next level.

From the standpoint of the *jiva*—individual consciousness—God is simultaneously transcendent and immanent, and the individual self is part of It (or Him or Her). This realization gives greater solace; that is, "I am part of Her, but how unfortunate that I don't experience it all the time!" At this next level, a longing takes hold of the seeker. Instead of reciting prayers and performing rituals, which the seeker did at the first level of dualistic realization, he or she finds prayers spontaneously flooding the mind and heart.

At this stage, although the aspirant doesn't experience oneness with the absolute, he or she does notice that the devotional relationship is beyond the level of the body. This devotion is a virtue of the heart, a condition of the mind. It needs a focus—an actual, conceivable object to which all thoughts and emotions can be channelled. Now the external God who used to dwell in the temple rushes to commune with the devotee right in the heart. Thus, God is not an external image but has become an indweller.

This is a personal relationship with an impersonal God. The impersonal God is infinite but what a wonder that He (or She) fits in this finite vessel of the body-mind. With this relationship as a support, an imperfect individual self tries to merge with the Beloved, who is perfect and universal. Before union occurs, the individual self feels that real joy would dawn only when the "part" that he or she is dissolves in the "whole" and becomes whole. The moment that happens, the oneness of jiva and Atman is experienced and there is no possibility thereafter of one loving the other because there is only One.

The first two stages described above are called the process of bhakti, but the last stage of experiencing oneness is simply the state of bhakti, which is all that remains. This is pure love—not the process of expressing it. However just as it is the nature of the ocean to express itself as waves, waves of love continually appear and subside from the ocean of unitary love.

It is only in the state of absolute *samadhi* that a yogi—a blessed devotee—experiences pure love without movement but when he or she comes back to outward consciousness, such a yogi prefers to enjoy a vibrant love. In the scriptures, this pure state of love is called *para bhakti*—the highest form of bhakti, while the first two levels are called *apara bhakti*, the lower form of bhakti. All are equally good and valid, in their rightful places and stages. This is the indescribable mystery of the transcendent reality.

9

Swami Rama of the Himalayas

The child of the Himalayas, Swami Rama is the contemporary link in the long lineage of the Himalayan sages and perhaps, the most significant figure among the known yogis who inhabit those mountains. He is the yogi, philosopher, and scientist who, through his master's blessing and his own untiring efforts, brought science and spirituality together, creating a bridge between East and West, and Indian philosophy and western psychology. Without disturbing the religious faith of either East or West, he introduced a perfect and practical method of bringing about the spiritual unfoldment and total well-being of all humankind.

Spiritual Training in Early Childhood

Swami Rama was born in the first quarter of the twentieth century in the Garhwal region of the Himalayas. Swamiji's extended family was known throughout the region, mainly due to the high positions the members held with the British government and the local king.

His father was famous for his knowledge of the scriptures and astrology. At one point in life, he became deeply withdrawn and after vacillating for several months, decided to renounce the world and live in seclusion because he was no longer happy living as a householder. He knew that his family would not approve of this idea so he left without asking his wife and other family members. After wandering for a few days, he arrived at the shrine known as Chandi Devi, near Haridwar. He made a dwelling near the shrine and began his intense *sadhana*. Six months passed.

One day a tall, thin, radiant yogi visited the shrine. At first glance Swamiji's father realized that this great man was his *gurudeva*. He greeted his master and received his blessing. As it turned out, this master was an adept of the Himalayas, the famous sage called Bengali Baba. Swamiji's father called him Babaji. Babaji stayed with Swamiji's father three days and taught him a systematic method of sadhana. Then he instructed his disciple to go home and live with his family, and soon he would be blessed with a child who would follow the path of light.

Swamiji's father returned home. One day while he was eating, Babaji appeared at the door and said, "Hari Om." Hearing his voice, Swamiji's father rushed to the door and fell at his master's feet. Rising, he asked his master to accept his hospitality but to his dismay, Babaji replied, "I have come not to accept your hospitality but rather, to take your son with me." The disciple replied, "You said that after I returned home, I would have a son. But so far it has not happened. Both my wife and I have grown old. If we have a child at this age, it will be a miracle. However if we do have one, he will be yours."

Soon after this conversation, Swamiji was born. A few days after his birth, Babaji returned and asked the new parents to give the infant to him. With a little hesitation, the mother put the child in Babaji's lap. Babaji looked at the mother put the child in Babaji's lap. Babaji looked at the infant, then gave him back to his mother saying, "Take care of him. When the time comes, I'll be back for him. Remember, he is my child, not yours."

While Swamiji was still quite young, his father died and soon after, Babaji took responsibility for raising him. Everyone in the family, including his mother, knew that this child would be well protected and that he could not get a better education than the one he would receive from Babaji.

Although Babaji was a swami without a family of his own, he knew more about raising children than any householder. He played the roles of mother, father, friend, and teacher to perfection. Along with spiritual and yogic training, Babaji saw that Swamiji was educated in established schools and colleges. However formal education was not the favorite part of Swamiji's life. The moment school was over, Swamiji eagerly returned to his master.

After early childhood had passed, Babaji began giving practical lessons on discipline and proper behavior. These lessons were difficult for Swamiji, who preferred to see a father, mother, and friend in Babaji rather than a teacher and disciplinarian. This was a constant source of uneasiness for Swamiji but it was great fun for Babaji. Occasionally Babaji brought him back to his birthplace to let him stay with the family. For Swamiji, this family had become strange. He did not feel any affinity with any of its members, including his mother. The moment his master left, he longed for his "real" father and mother—Babaji—and cried to go back. After a few such incidents, he completely overcame his emotional ties to his biological family and became totally adjusted to life with his master.

His master preferred to live in seclusion. His favorite dwellings were the caves and huts situated in the high mountains, usually in the areas of Tungnath, Badrinath, Kedarnath, and Gangotri in the northern Himalayas and near Kathmandu, all the way to Darjeeling in the Kinchanchunga ranges of the eastern Himalayas. Sometimes during the winter, he travelled to the shrines that lie in the Vindhaya range, which stretches from central India to the southern peninsula. During his travels with his master, Swamiji was exposed to a wide range of spiritual teachers and seekers.

Babaji knew that there was only one person in Swamiji's life—himself. In Babaji, Swamiji found several people— mother, father, brother, friend, and teacher. For the overall development of his personality, Swamiji needed to interact with all these people. However for spiritual training, the teacher's role was paramount, and for that role to become dominant, a gradual withdrawing from the other roles was necessary. Babaji began this process by sending Swamiji to one of his disciples in the majestic Gangotri region of the Himalayas.

Swamiji's spiritual brother was known by the name Swami Shivananda or Gangotri Wale (not to be confused with the Swami Shivananda of the Divine Light Society). Swami Shivananda was quite learned and was one of his master's most advanced disciples. As instructed by Babaji, he started teaching Swamiji the actual disciplines that one needs on the path of spiritual unfoldment, as well as the scriptures.

Swami Shivananda loved Swamiji but the training required that he be tough with this young student. Poor Swamiji could not understand how his brother, who loved him so much, could be so hard on him. There were times when the argumentative and rebellious part of Swamiji came forward and he refused to be disciplined, even by his own *gurubhai* (spiritual brother). Although Swami Shivananda was a man of depthless wisdom, patience, endurance, and tolerance, he occasionally became fed up with Swamiji and sent him back to his master. When this happened Babaji would at first display his limitless compassion, mildly

Dandi Swami Sri Shivananda Saraswati of Gangotri

agreeing that Swamiji had not done anything wrong. But after a couple of days Babaji would remind him that obstinacy, lack of discipline, and disrespect for your teacher—who is the source of knowledge—can prevent an aspirant from advancing spiritually. Like a loving parent, first Babaji gave Swamiji a gentle hint. Then, he advised him like a friend. Finally like a teacher, he emphatically instructed Swamiji to go back to Swami Shivananda and behave properly. In this way, Swamiji passed his early and preteen years, studying and practicing with his master and Swami Shivanandaji.

By the time Swamiji reached his preteen years, he was perfectly adjusted to a monastic, ascetic life. The world, which appears so real to us, made very little sense to him. The pure spiritual life requires discipline, for it has its own rules, laws, and standards. Because those who enter spiritual life come from the world, they carry *samskaras*, which must be washed off or totally burned if they are to enjoy the beauty and joy of monastic life. For this reason, while Swamiji was still a teenager, his master guided him in undertaking powerful spiritual disciplines to burn even the subtlest seeds of previous samskaras. One of the practices he undertook was *gayatri purascharna*.

Intense Meditation on the Gayatri Mantra

Babaji brought Swamiji to the holy city of Benares and instructed him to complete a specific course of meditation while living in solitude. His master found a place outside the city, on the other side of the Ganga, where he built a hut near the bank. He drew a line with purificatory and protective mantras (*lakshmana rekha*) and instructed Swamiji not to cross that line except to perform his morning and evening ablutions. Further, his master specifically instructed Swamiji that throughout this period of practice, he must not pay attention to anything or anyone outside the line. "No matter what goes on outside the line, it's

none of your business. Pay attention to your practice and
be aware of your goal the whole time."

Swamiji made his fire (*dhuni*), which was to be his only
friend, night and day, facing the Ganga under a small
thatched roof extending over the door of the hut. A *pandit*
from the city, who was a disciple of Swamiji's master, was
assigned to provide food once a day. Swamiji was sup-
posed to complete 2.4 million repetitions of the *gayatri
mantra* in 16 months.

He began the practice. A few months passed and people
from the city came to know about this young, vibrant
brahmachari (at that time Swamiji had not yet been initiated into the Swami order). Many learned and wealthy
people began visiting him. They noticed how one-pointedly
he was engaged in his practice and how calm and tranquil
he was, on one hand, and how vibrant and energetic, on
the other. They were impressed by his dedication to spiritual life at such an early age. Those who saw Swamiji even
once, talked about him constantly, and his popularity
spread. The less attention Swamiji paid to visitors, the
more visitors were impressed with this uninvolved and indifferent *sadhu*.

This made a group of pandits jealous and they began
criticizing him: "He's just a young boy. He should have
gone to school and learned something about life and the
scriptures."

"He's a fake. He's just trying to impress others and become popular. Otherwise he would have done his *tapas*
(austerities) somewhere else. . ." Swamiji did not react.

One day when he had been doing his practice for
eleven months, a group of people who were determined
to disturb him got together and made a plan. They approached Swamiji and challenged him to a debate. When
he remained silent, they persisted. Suddenly he lost his
temper, crossed the boundary line, caught hold of
someone's neck, and pushed him toward the Ganga. This

frightened the hecklers who promptly dispersed. Soon afterward, the pandit who was supplying him with food and
other necessities appeared and handed Swamiji a telegram
from his master. The telegram read, "You ruined your
practice. Start over."

With a strong resolve not to commit such a mistake
again, Swamiji began once more. Again, almost an entire
year passed and the time for testing arrived. One night,
around midnight, a dwarf came and sat in front of the fire,
keeping outside the boundary line so that there was a
good distance between himself and Swamiji. Neither
broke the silence. The dwarf stayed almost two hours. The
next night, he came again at exactly the same time and sat
there, just as he had the night before. Night after night,
the dwarf visited Swamiji without disturbing him.

One night Swamiji asked the dwarf who he was and
where he came from. The dwarf answered. The next night,
Swamiji extended the interaction even further, saying he
had a desire to eat *jalebi* (an Indian sweet) and asking if
the dwarf could get it for him. The dwarf responded enthusi-
astically, saying that he would get it immediately. Swamiji
objected, thinking there were two obstacles—the man was
a dwarf and there were no boats to take him across the
Ganga in the middle of the night. But the dwarf left, insisting that he knew a place where he could easily get jalebi
and milk. He returned with the sweets and the milk before
3 A.M. Swamiji enjoyed the treat.

From then on the dwarf came every night, bringing
jalebi and milk. Soon the pandit, who always brought
Swamiji food at midday, began wondering why there were
always leftovers. When he asked why he was not eating
properly, Swamiji told him about the dwarf and how he
brought jalebi and milk every night. The pandit was surprised and asked who the dwarf was, where and how he
lived, and so on. He was concerned about Swamiji and did
not want him to get into any trouble.

When the dwarf appeared that night with the jalebi and milk, Swamiji asked his name and address. The dwarf told him. The next day Swamiji gave this information to the pandit, who went to that address but found only a ruined dwelling. When he made inquiries in the vicinity, he found out that ninety years before, someone with the name the dwarf had given Swamiji—a learned pandit who was also a dwarf—had lived in the ruined house.

The next day the pandit told Swamiji that there was no such person living at that address. Taunting Swamiji, he said, "Brahmachariji, how can a person who died ninety years ago feed you jalebi and milk? And for what reason? There is no need of playing tricks. Tell me what's wrong with you. Have you lost your appetite or is someone feeding you and you do not want to tell me who?"

That night the dwarf came and sat down in his usual manner, well away from both the fire and Swamiji. Swamiji demanded that the dwarf tell him his real name, his true address, and his purpose in visiting exactly at midnight. The dwarf replied, "You are doing your job and I'm doing mine. I never disturb you and by serving you, I do my work the way I am instructed to."

Upon hearing this answer, several thoughts flashed through Swamiji's mind. "Is he not human? Can a person who died long ago materialize himself and be visible? Is this just a trick of my mind? He can be seen, but can he be touched?" As these thoughts flashed through his mind, Swamiji became enraged—not only at the dwarf's behavior but at the whole situation. In a fit of anger he poured a few drops of water on his right palm. While repeating the gayatri mantra, he raised his hand to the dwarf and ordered, "Tell me who you are or I'll destroy you." The dwarf did not move. Swamiji shouted, demanding once again to know who he was. Still the dwarf remained silent. Losing his temper, Swamiji threw the water on the dwarf. Instantly, the dwarf vanished. At once, Swamiji realized he had made another mistake. He was disappointed and felt sorry for himself.

The next day the pandit came with a message from his master, "You have ruined your practice again, my son. Be strong and conquer these negative and destructive tendencies. Bless you."

Swamiji began the practice a third time. This time, through the grace of his master, he completed it. Recounting this incident years later, Swamiji said, "These tendencies keep coming up until they are completely conquered. It's not an easy task but neither is it impossible. Blessed are those who make sincere efforts to work with themselves at every level. And even more blessed are those who follow an authentic system of sadhana under the guidance of a competent master. Some attain victory relatively easily and quickly. Others become exhausted. Those who give up become stranded. But those who, faced with failure and exhaustion, surrender themselves to the Lord, the Master—for them, the final hurdle is removed once and for all."

In addition to teaching Swamiji and helping him undergo these practices, his master created an environment that allowed Swamiji to gain a wide range of experiences. He made Swamiji travel from cave to cave and monastery to monastery, visiting the adepts of all traditions.

A glimpse of Swamiji's untiring journey and his meeting with different sages can be found in his account of his life, *Living with the Himalayan Masters*. As is apparent from the experiences chronicled in that book, the lessons he got from different masters added fuel to his burning desire to know the truth at every level. Every experience, whether pleasant or unpleasant, helped him understand how the stream of life is filled with numberless and mysterious currents and cross-currents. Knowing the stream of life requires knowledge of these various currents. Nothing can be done unless someone stands on the firm ground of *vairagya* (non-attachment). From this ground, one can dive deep, gather the pearls of wisdom, and return to the safety of the same firm ground.

Preparation for Becoming a Swami

As Swamiji underwent these intensive spiritual practices under the guidance of his master, his desire to attain the highest state of Self-realization became more intense. He repeatedly asked his master to initiate him in the path of renunciation, *sanyasa*, but his master kept avoiding the request. Following the exhortations of the scriptures, his master insisted that he should renounce the world only after he had come to understand it thoroughly. Without a direct experience of the unfulfilling nature of worldly objects, which makes the charms and temptations of the world meaningless, the path of renunciation is neither safe nor easy.

His master said, "In order to connect and establish yourself completely 'there,' you must first free yourself from the fetters 'here.' The greater part of sadhana consists of crossing the mire of illusion. That's where the effort is needed. The knowledge of the truth is self-evident and is a matter of revelation, which occurs instantly and spontaneously. Unless you are completely fed up with the deceptive nature of this world, worldly people, and worldly activities, you will not have an unwavering, one-pointed commitment to attaining the highest goal. Therefore, my son, look closely at this world—especially the things that appear to be glamorous and those that seem indispensable to your survival, the people who claim to love you, people who are famous, and people who appear to be virtuous and powerful. Do not search for faults in others but sharpen your intellect and gain maturity so that you do not become trapped in this world."

Following the instructions of his master, Swamiji traveled widely throughout India, visiting rich and poor, the educated and illiterate, social reformers and businessmen, and religious leaders and politicians. He encountered intellectuals and great saints, adept yogis and preachers. There were times when people admired him and other times when people ridiculed and condemned him. At times he mistook a magician for an accomplished saint. Once he mistook an adept in deep *samadhi* for someone who had fallen asleep. These experiences helped him become sharp in the worldly sense and wise in the spiritual sense.

Gold in the Turban

On the path of spirituality one must gain the ability to distinguish between appearance and reality. When Swamiji was still a brahmachari (an apprentice swami), he came down from the mountains and stayed at Rishikesh, in the foothills of the Himalayas. In those days there was nothing in Rishikesh except a few ashrams and a small police station. In isolated places, *sadhus* lived in their small huts. Not too far away from the place where Swamiji has his ashram today, there was a banyan tree (which is still standing in front of the Kali Kamali Ka Ashram). Under this tree Swamiji prepared his dhuni (fire) and fixed his asana (the place for sitting and meditating).

Shortly thereafter, a sadhu known as Pagri Wale Baba (a sadhu who wears a turban) arrived at Rishikesh, followed by a crowd. People believed he had a *siddhi* (a supernatural power) that was somehow connected to his turban, for he never took it off. His ability to live comfortably without ever taking off his turban gave credibility to his claim that he had conquered the concerns of heat and cold, comfort and discomfort. People from all over flocked to see him and receive his blessing but Swamiji paid no attention. After a time, several other sadhus attempted to persuade Swamiji to visit this holy man who, in their opinion, had blessed Rishikesh with his arrival.

Swamiji responded gently, "I pray to the divinity in everyone—in you and in him. But I am fine right here with my dhuni."

A few days later, word of Swamiji's indifference reached Pagri Wale Baba, who was apparently quite upset by it. He demanded that Swamiji come and see him. This time Swamiji refused outright, without showing even the slightest respect. The sadhu was enraged. Accompanied by his followers, he came to Swamiji. By chance when he arrived, Swamiji was sitting in his asana, the meditative pose.

It was Swamiji's custom not to get up until he had completed his meditation (except in honor of his master, should he happen to come by). Therefore without disturbing his meditative pose, he offered a piece of jute cloth as a seat for his visitor but the sadhu demanded that he rise and greet him with the traditional courtesy. Swamiji explained that he was required to remain in his asana but Pagri Wale Baba kept insisting. Finally, to everyone's surprise, Swamiji scolded the sadhu, telling him to sit down and prove that he was not a robber.

Then Swamiji looked at the crowd and asked, "How many of you are the disciples of this robber? Just wait, I'm going to turn him over to the police." Everyone in the crowd was shocked and waited to see what would happen next. Swamiji told them, "He robbed a widow and took all her gold jewelry, which he keeps in his turban. That is why this turban *baba* never takes off his turban."

Hearing this, half the crowd went away immediately because they were afraid of being arrested. Some of those who remained said, "I'm not his disciple. I was just passing by."

"My brother was his disciple and that's how I heard about him."

"I also suspected that he might not be a genuine sadhu."

Swamiji instructed someone to ride his bicycle to the police station and get the police. When they arrived, the police made Pagri Wale Baba take off his turban. They found that it was full of gold and they led him away to jail.

Soon after, Swamiji left Rishikesh but this incident led people to say among themselves that this young man has *divya chaksu*, the inner eyes. When the older sadhus investigated, they found that Swamiji was the beloved disciple of Bengali Baba, the adept from the high mountains.

How Swamiji knew that this sadhu was a fake, he alone knows. But the lesson this incident conveys to us is that in respect to spiritual wisdom, how big a turban someone wears, how long a beard a man grows, how eye-catching the clothes, how many disciples he trails behind him, how many ashrams he has established is all immaterial. A seeker of truth must remember that this world is full of such people and only one who seeks diligently and fearlessly finds the genuine teacher. Others—those who are fooled by appearances—will waste their time.

Initiation into Sanyasa

After going through a number of such experiences and gaining knowledge of the world, Swamiji became fully prepared to be initiated as a *sanyasi*, a renunciate. The world and things of the world had become too little for him. Swamiji was ordained as a *dandi* swami (the highest order of sanyasa), which is symbolized by a *danda*, a staff that a swami of this order carries all the time. Along with the danda come strict spiritual disciplines and observances. His master said, "God bless you. Now you are a swami, the master of yourself. You are free to create your own destiny because all your previous karmic bonds have been offered into the fire."

After this initiation, Swamiji had the astounding experiences of receiving *purna patra* (the bowl that is ever-filled with food) from the Ganga, visiting his grandmaster in Tibet, witnessing *parakaya pravesha* (casting off the body voluntarily), and learning the esoteric sciences such as *surya vijnana* and *shrividya*, all of which he relates in *Living with the Himalayan Masters.*

On the Banks of the Narmada

When he returned from Tibet in 1948, Swamiji was instructed to intensify his practice while living on the banks of the Narmada. Accordingly he made his dwelling on the river bank, well away from human settlements and began his meditation. Except for a few villagers who brought him the bare necessities, Swamiji was in complete solitude and able to do his sadhana without attracting any notice.

One day an amazing thing happened. A group of hunters chasing their prey through the forest arrived at the river bank where, to their astonishment, they saw a man sitting quietly with his eyes closed, surrounded by crocodiles. They were intrigued by the fact that neither the man nor the crocodiles showed any fear. They knew that this was not a safe place to stay because it was a spot where many wild animals came to drink, so they took a few pictures of this man and the crocodiles and departed.

The next day the photos were all over the newspapers in nearby towns, and people began searching for Swamiji. Not very many people were successful in reaching him but those who were spread the story further. Eventually this tale reached the ears of Dr. Kurtkoti, the Shankaracharya of Karvirapitham. Dr. Kurtkoti, a learned scholar and social reformer, was highly respected. Hoping to retire, he was searching for the person who could meet all the requirements necessary to hold this spiritual seat. This man who had accidently been exposed to the camera intrigued him so he appointed a group of pandits to visit Swamiji and find out how he lived, what he did, and what daily routine he followed.

The pandits saw that this young, solitary sadhu sat in meditation for several hours without the slightest movement in his asana, that he hardly slept at night, spoke very

Sri Swami Rama on the banks of the Narmada

little, and interacted only with the villager who occasionally brought him food and milk. They had a few brief conversations with him, which gave them some idea of the depth of his knowledge.

When Dr. Kurtkoti had gathered as much information as he could, he approached Swamiji himself and proposed that he accept the position of Shankaracharya. Swamiji replied that he would do so only with the permission of his master. His master granted permission and in 1949, Swamiji was installed in the seat of Shankaracharya of Karvirapitham. At the time, Swamiji was known by the name of Sadashiva Bharati.

Tenure as Shankaracharya

Swamiji did not know what he was stepping into. The coronation was publicized worldwide, a fact that Swamiji discovered only when he began to receive letters and telegrams from religious leaders everywhere, as well as from world leaders, heads of state, and countless others. The coronation ceremony lasted for more than a month. One day Dr. Kurtkoti handed all of his official correspondence over to Swamiji, along with all of his responsibilities.

Before becoming Shankaracharya, Swamiji had lived with Mahatma Gandhi, Tagore, and Sri Aurobindo, all of whom were powerful free thinkers, social reformers, and political leaders. These experiences and his travels throughout the country had helped him to develop a broad understanding of the social, cultural, and economic aspects of Indian society. In addition, his concept of religion and spirituality was also wider than that of typical Indian swamis.

As Shankaracharya, Swamiji had the power to reform Hindu society. He took an active part in the noble work of social reform that Dr. Kurtkoti had begun. One of the most important of these projects was the campaign to educate the oppressed members of Indian society (the untouchables) and bring them into the mainstream, giving them the right to enter temples and worship God just as members of the so-called upper class did.

Another of his projects was abolishing the custom of *devadasi*. Devadasis were women who lived in temples, mostly in south India. They spent their lives serving the priests by cleaning the temples and giving music and dance performances as part of the daily worship. Although they were not allowed to marry, they bore children who were raised in the temples as orphans. These women were constantly being abused and had become slaves to the temple and the priests who ran them.

Swamiji brought these two injustices to the attention of the politicians and members of the upper class. The greatest challenge he faced was from the orthodox brahmins, to whom the concept of change and reformation was anathema. However after a long struggle, he succeeded in making reforms.

In spite of this, his life at the ashram grew heavier and more confining as time passed. As head of the *pitham* (ashram), he was expected to fulfill all the duties established by the tradition as well as the time-honored customs that had grown up around this position over the centuries. For example he was expected to be a great yogi, guide students, give discourses, and create and maintain an environment conducive to the spiritual growth of the ashramites. He also was required to allow himself to be worshipped by his devotees as a living shrine. Even his daily routine was ritualized. Someone had to give him his bath, and after he had put on his clothes and customary ornaments, he had to sit on a throne where people could come and have his *darshana* (glance). All day long, people came offering flowers, sweets, prostrating at his feet, and seeking his blessings. All this left very little time for his meditation.

Swamiji realized that it was not easy to do selfless service and yet enjoy peace of mind. He missed his solitude, his peaceful nights, and his two best friends meditation and his most beloved master. He realized that in order for an ashram to be truly spiritual, people first must be taught to distinguish spirituality from religious beliefs, customs, dogmas, and superstitions. It appeared that Indian society was not yet ready to embrace higher values of spirituality, and he knew it was a waste of time to work with those who are not prepared. It was time for him to return to the Himalayas.

Swamiji realized he was trapped. People would not allow him to leave openly so he would have to find another way to get out. Usually he was not allowed even to walk alone but one day he somehow managed to get into his car undetected. He drove to the nearby city of Jabalpur and parked the car near the police station with a note, "Please return this car to Karvirapitham." Then he walked to the railway station. He had left most of his official garments in the ashram but he still had his staff and the sandals, both of which were trimmed in gold. Almost anyone would recognize these things as the trappings of the Shankaracharya.

Swamiji boarded the express train for Allahabad, sitting in a seat reserved for someone else. He told the passengers sitting next to him that he did not have a ticket and offered to yield his seat to the rightful owner. But Swamiji's appearance was so imposing that the actual owner hesitated to step forward. After the train left the station, the conductor came to collect the tickets. Swamiji said that he would buy the ticket and pay the penalty when he reached Allahabad where his friends were waiting. The conductor insisted on knowing who he was but Swamiji said only, "Please do not ask here. Help me to reach Allahabad."

The conductor obliged, accompanying him to Allahabad where he found out that Swamiji was the Shankaracharya. Swamiji stayed with his students in Allahabad for a few days and then travelled to the Himalayas to meet his master.

Once reunited with his master, this chapter in his life was closed. However out in the world, people continued searching for him. When they found no trace, several hypotheses arose: he was no longer alive; he was hiding somewhere; he had gone abroad; or he was totally absorbed in intense practices somewhere deep in the interior of the forests or the mountains.

A Decade of Intense Practice

This last conjecture was closest to the truth. Only a select group of people know about this particular period of his life, which Swamiji dedicated to intense sadhana. He occasionally says that these were the best years of his life. He traveled with his master to remote places known only to the *hansas*, the adepts living in the high mountains. Completely free of the world outside, he enjoyed the exclusive company of the Himalayas and the Himalayan adepts. Old sadhus still remember when he lived in remote places such as Gangotri, Tarkeshwar, and Uttarkashi—holy shrines that lie in the deep recesses of the majestic mountains. There were also times when he stayed far away from these holy shrines, which were often visited by pilgrims. With no belongings, not even a water pot, he lived as an *avadhoota*, a sadhu who maintains a practice of extreme non-possessiveness (*aparighraha*). As an avadhoota sadhu, he made no effort to find food but when villagers heard he was living in nearby forests, they would find him and give him food. Swamiji's other favorite jaunts in those days were the forests in the Satna district of Madhya Pradesh, Chitrakut, and Vindyachal.

After this period he returned to the foothills and plains, staying mainly in Allahabad, Kanpur, and Rishikesh. Once again his master instructed him to undergo an intense meditation practice, one which required him to stay day and night in a particular cave. Swamiji lived in that cave for eleven months without seeing a single human being. As he writes in his autobiography, this is an essential practice in our tradition. After undergoing this practice, it is believed that even the most inert aspirant will realize the highest truth. Because the aspirant is not allowed to come out and take a bath, Swamiji took a prana bath by practicing vigorous breathing exercises. We do not know exactly how the advanced yogis do this but Swamiji has demonstrated it on several occasions. He simply sits down, closes his eyes, and concentrates (probably at the naval center). Within minutes he begins to perspire profusely, opening the pores and eliminating wastes.

During these eleven months in the cave, Swamiji ate a small amount of food once a day. His diet consisted of barley, mountain vegetables, some juices, and a glass of milk. He practiced hatha yoga and pranayama regularly and slept only two or three hours each day. The entrance of the cave was closed but there was an outlet in the back for waste to wash away. A tiny hole in the ceiling of the cave admitted a single beam of light. This beam was meant to help concentrate the mind on a single point. In such a strict environment, either you really meditate and enjoy it or you quickly become imbalanced and quit the practice. A real taste for silence unfolds after maintaining a deep state of meditation.

When he had completed the practice, Swamiji came out of the cave and to his surprise, the world looked entirely different. He had difficulty adjusting and had to reorient himself. This took several weeks but even after he had done so, he maintained this realization: "The world is a theater in which one can test one's inner strength, speech, emotions, thoughts, and behaviors."

Journey to the West

Soon after he had completed this practice, Swamiji's master instructed him to go to the West, saying, "You have a mission to complete and a message to deliver. That message is ours and you are my instrument."

Following his master's instructions, Swamiji left for Tokyo. When he arrived, a stranger approached him and asked him where he'd come from and where he would be staying.

Swamiji replied, "I have a friend and I will stay with him."

"Who is your friend?" inquired the stranger.

Because Swamiji did not know anyone in Japan, he said, "You are that friend."

Swamiji stayed with this gentleman who later introduced him to Yokadasan, the spiritual head of Mahikari. When they met, Yokadasan hugged Swamiji and said, "I have been waiting for you. I hope you will give me the secret teachings of the Himalayan masters."

Swamiji shared his master's message with Yokadasan. Six months later he left for the United States.

Before he left India Swamiji's master had told him that he would meet his students and associates in the United States, where he had to complete his mission: creating a bridge between East and West and between spirituality and science.

He arrived in the United States in 1969 and, just as his master had promised, a highly educated core of students soon collected around him. His interaction with scientists, medical doctors, and psychologists began when he was invited by Dr. Elmer and Mrs. Alyce Green to the Menninger Foundation in Topeka, Kansas. As reported in *Science Year: The World Book Science Annual,* published in 1974, Swamiji demonstrated an astounding feat of "mind over matter." Under strict laboratory conditions witnessed by seven scientists, Swamiji caused a 14-inch aluminum knitting needle mounted horizontally on a vertical shaft five feet away from him, to rotate ten degrees towards him as he focused his gaze on the needle. At the time of the experiment, Swamiji's mouth and nose were covered by a plastic mask. He was breathing through foam rubber so that his breath could not affect the needle in any way.

In that same laboratory Swamiji's brain waves, heart beat, respiration, skin resistance, muscle tension, blood flow in the hands, and hand temperature were recorded. By using the power of the mind, Swamiji made the temperature of the little finger side of his right palm differ from the temperature of the thumb side of the same hand by 10 degrees Fahrenheit. Later Swamiji also demonstrated that he could radically alter his heart rate and produce specific brain waves at will. When people asked how he did such things, he explained that such phenomena are possible because, "All of the body is in the mind but not all of the mind is in the body." The body follows the dictates of the mind.

By demonstrating his yogic powers, Swamiji excited the curiosity of scientists and opened new dimensions in the field of parapsychology. However his mission was not confined to a limited field of learning or merely to helping write another chapter in the history of medicine and psychology. His ultimate goal was to introduce the West to the path of spirituality and total well-being, which had been discovered by the ancient sages and which had helped millions throughout the ages.

Swamiji traveled throughout the United States and Canada, conducting lectures and workshops. Within a year, he founded The Himalayan International Institute of Yoga Science and Philosophy. At this Institute Swamiji taught a system of holistic living, which he based on the philosophy and practices of yoga and vedanta, two major streams of Eastern philosophy and spirituality. Through the grace of his master and his own untiring efforts, he prepared a group of students who later began to share their knowledge by teaching all over the country. Swamiji's approach to spirituality in modern times is unique in the sense that it is completely unaffected by religious dogma and cultural biases, it is scientifically verifiable, and it is equally useful to everyone, regardless of whether they live in the East or in the West.

While teaching in the West Swamiji always kept his master's words in his mind, transmitting them to his students. His master had said that people living in both the East and the West had the same purpose in life although they differ from each other in approach. Neither people in the East nor the West have found a perfect path so far—they are still conducting experiments in the right ways of living. In the words of his master, "The message of the Himalayan masters is timeless and has nothing to do with the primitive concepts of East or West. Extremes will not help humanity to attain the higher step of civilization for which we all are striving. Inner strength, cheerfulness, and selfless service are the basic principles of life. It is immaterial whether one lives in the East or West. A human being should be a human being first. A real human being is a member of the cosmos. Geographical boundaries have no power to divide humanity. . . . All spiritual practices should be verified scientifically if science has the capacity to do so."

A Glimpse of Swamiji's Teachings

The following material was gleaned from Swamiji's writings, lectures, and private conversations with his students.

Seeker: What is the purpose of life?

Swamiji: The purpose of life is to know yourself at every level. A human being is neither body nor mind alone. A human being is also a breathing being. The body and mind are held together with the power of the pranic force. Breath is the major manifestation of that pranic force. As long as a human is breathing, he or she is alive. The breath creates a link between the body and mind. It works like a customs officer, registering everything that is exported and imported from either side.

To keep a harmonious balance between the body and

mind, you must pay attention to how you breathe. Healthy breathing is the foundation for securing the health of both the body and mind. In order to achieve the next level of health and happiness, you must work not only with the body or mind but also with the breath. According to the Upanishads, the breath is like a queen bee. The body and mind with all their organs and faculties follow this queen bee.

After knowing the dynamics of physical well-being and securing it, you come to realize that true happiness does not come from the body. Happiness is the creation of mind. An unhealthy body can create obstacles in achieving peace and happiness but a healthy body contributes very little to happiness. It is the mind which has to be made healthy, which has to be disciplined and brought under control. Breath is the key to accomplishing this. The obstacles that may arise from the physical level of one's being can be prevented by living in a holistic manner—eating a balanced diet, practicing yogic exercises, regulating the four primitive urges (eating, sleeping, sex, and self-preservation), and going to bed and waking up on schedule.

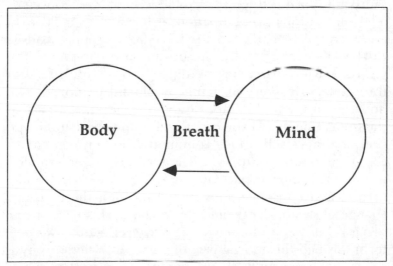

Relationship Among Body, Breath, and Mind

The degree of health and physical strength you gain by following this holistic lifestyle can be refined and advanced by practicing pranayama. When the aspirant is advanced enough to practice pranayama, he or she has the ability to notice subtler causes of disturbance that arise directly from the mind. This is the time when the aspirant must make a commitment to the inward journey—the practice of meditation.

After making some initial efforts to meditate and noticing a good degree of improvement, the student may experience unconscious memories and habit patterns springing up from the depths of the unconscious mind. At this juncture, the student cannot escape (nor is there a need to escape) from his or her own unconscious material. With the help of the systematic practice of meditation and contemplation, the aspirant can dive deeply within and explore the subtle causes of habit patterns, previously unknown to the conscious mind. The student learns to penetrate through the unconscious mind with the help of vairagya (non-attachment), thereby attaining freedom from those samskaras once and for all. A mind free from all conscious and unconscious preoccupations is like a clear mirror. In this mirror, Atman, the inner self, is reflected spontaneously.

The knowers of truth, those who have completed the entire journey from beginning to end, divide life into three categories: mortal, semi-mortal, and immortal. The body, breath, and conscious mind are the mortal part of the human being. At the other end of the spectrum is the soul, the inner self, which is immortal. In between comes the unconscious mind, which is semi-mortal or semi-immortal. The mortal part of our being—that is the body, breath, and conscious mind—goes through the constant change of death, decay, and destruction. This part of our being is born and one day dies. Whatever actions we perform through this mortal part of ourselves, whether physical, verbal, or mental, create an impression in the uncon-

scious mind. All such impressions are stored in the form
of samskaras in the unconscious mind, from where they
motivate our mind, senses, and body to undertake certain
actions.

This vicious cycle never ends unless we apply the techniques of spiritual discipline. At the time of death when
the body and conscious mind fall apart, a human being is
still alive, dwelling in the unconscious. The samskaras of
unfulfilled desires force the unconscious to beg nature to
provide a new body. Thus a human being goes through
the process of rebirth.

Once you attain freedom from the samskaras stored in
the unconscious, semi-mortal part of your being, you realize that you are pure Atman, the eternal self, which is subject
to neither birth nor death. Such a realized person is "immortal." It is only lack of knowledge that keeps this immortal self involved in the cycle of birth and death, where
it falls victim to fear concerning its so-called "mortality."

Seeker: Then it seems that a person must work with the
samskaras—the subtle, motivating, powerful seeds that remain
dormant in the unconscious mind. How is it possible to
attain freedom from these samskaras?

Swamiji: Discipline is the answer. No matter which path
you follow, no matter which practice you undergo, and no
matter which tradition you belong to, you need a disciplined mind. *A confused mind is not fit to follow any path.*

Whether you stay at home and pursue your sadhana or
renounce your home, you have to face your deep-rooted
samskaras. It takes a long time to get rid of them. Therefore do not be disappointed when you find you cannot attain
freedom from your samskaras during a month-long retreat.
Have patience and keep on working. Cleansing and replac-
ing the mental content is possible when you follow a systematic path of self-discipline.

Stay away from teachers and preachers who profess to
teach spirituality and meditation without also teaching

discipline. No matter how sound their techniques, unless the student is trained to become disciplined, it is like sowing seeds in an untilled, barren field.

All you need is to look at the totality of your life, set your priorities, and create a bridge between life within and without. Discipline is the bedrock of that bridge.

Seeker: Does one attain the highest goal, self-realization, through self-effort, God's grace, or a combination of both?

Swamiji: In the final analysis, it happens through God's grace. However, relying on God's grace and abandoning self-effort, especially in the initial stage of the inward journey, is a big mistake. God's grace is like rain that falls over a vast area without any regard for which particular areas will benefit from it. It rains on the unjust and the just alike. Even after it rains, the land that is not permeable and cannot hold the waters, or land that is infertile or without seeds, remains barren. But a fertile land thrives where seeds have been sown and precautions have been taken to make the best use of the rainfall. Plants grow and flowers bloom. So it is with our own preparedness to receive grace, assimilate it, and benefit from it.

When you have made all possible efforts with full sincerity and have become exhausted, then you cry out in despair. This sort of cry is the highest form of *bhakti*. The result will be real ecstasy. This highest state of ecstasy is called God's grace. Grace is the fruit that you receive from your faithful and sincere efforts.

In yogic literature, receiving grace is known as receiving *shaktipata*. Shaktipata is possible with a prepared student who has gone through a long period of discipline, austerity, and spiritual practice. It is a natural unfoldment of divine grace. In order to attain the highest realization, four types of grace have to converge on one point: *shastra kripa*, the grace of the scriptures; *atma kripa*, the grace of oneself; *guru kripa*, the grace of the guru; and *Ishwara kripa*, the grace of God.

Through shastra kripa, the grace of the scriptures, you gain an intellectual understanding of the higher dimensions of life, become inspired, gather courage to follow the path of light, and overcome your trivial concerns and doubts. Then you need atma kripa, the grace of your Self, which takes the form of committing yourself to the practice. Sincerity, regularity, staying away from useless things and useless people, and being strong with one's decision is atma kripa.

Once you have attained these two graces, you are destined to receive guru kripa, the grace of the guru. That is why it is said, "When the student is ready, the guru appears." And once you receive guru kripa, which is totally unconditional (from the standpoint of the guru), the grace of God follows automatically. In fact guru kripa itself turns into God's grace.

Behind this four-fold grace, there is only one functioning force: *karuna*—compassion—the unconditional love of the divine for all individual souls. From the standpoint of sadhana, this internal and ever-flowing stream of divine compassion manifests in the form of this four-fold grace, leading sincere aspirants to the highest goal.

Seeker: If I study carefully and do my practices sincerely and faithfully, will I receive guidance directly from within? Or are instructions and guidance from a guru in human form absolutely necessary?

Swamiji: You need an external guru to attain the guru within. Sometimes you may become egotistical and decide, "I do not need a guru." That is ego talking. In your search if you are not careful, you may become too intellectual and ignore your spontaneous intuition. Or you may become too emotional and ignore your reason. Both situations are equally dangerous. Furthermore the past several thousand years have produced a vast literature on spirituality. Often novice seekers become confused about which practices they should do and which teachings or practices should be ignored. As long as you study one path or discipline to the exclusion of others, the teachings seem sound. But when you compare and contrast them with other teachings, you become confused. That is where you need a guru, a spiritual instructor who has attained realization while following the path that he or she is teaching you.

Seeker: It is said that it is not easy to find a *sadguru*, a spiritual master. And without a real master, how is it possible to receive true guidance?

Swamiji: A good student can never meet a bad guru, but the reverse is also true. Similar attracts similar. If for some reason, the "dissimilar" meet, the higher force intervenes and drives away those who are unprepared. Do not worry about who is good and who is bad. Increase your capacity. Purify yourself. Acquire the gentle strength within. God will come and say to you, "I want to enter this living temple that you are." Prepare yourself for that situation. Remove the impurities and you will find that he who wants to know reality is himself the source of reality.

Seeker: How do yogis view the phenomenon of death?

Swamiji: Death is a habit of the body, a necessary change. Unfortunately while we are alive, we don't pay attention to the importance of knowing how to die at will, nor do we prepare ourselves psychologically for this moment. People think that death is painful but in fact it's not death, but rather the fear of death, that creates misery for a dying person.

From the moment of birth, we constantly tell ourselves that the objects of the world are real and that our happiness and completion depends on material possessions. There comes a time when we notice that the material objects we've acquired are drastically changing and falling apart, and that the same thing is happening with our relationships. We become disappointed with life. A sense of insecurity begins to grow concerning the life hereafter. At the same time we become deeply attached to our children and possessions.

Just as we have discovered ways to prepare the expect-
ant mother to have a safe birth and minimize the pain during labor, we must learn the techniques of casting off the
body without fear and pain. The brain has a limited capacity to sense physical pain, because at a certain point it becomes oblivious to physical pain. Thus during death, a
person does not suffer from physical pain as much as he
or she experiences psychological pain. A dying person becomes lonely and frightened.

Yogis have discovered several methods of casting off their
bodies voluntarily and joyfully. There are many signs and
symptoms of impending death. An evolved yogi intuitively
knows precisely when and at what time it will happen and
greets that moment joyfully, casting off the body in the
same way that ordinary human beings take off their
clothes.

Some of the famous yogic techniques for casting off the
body are *hima-samadhi*, casting off one's body in deep
snow; *jala-samadhi*, casting off one's body in water; and
sthala-samadhi, casting off one's body while sitting in
siddhasana (the accomplished pose) and consciously opening the fontanelle. Two of the most highly regarded methods of casting off the body are by meditating on the solar
plexus and reducing the body to ashes in a fraction of a
second or by piercing the *brahma-randhra*, also known as
the *brahma nadi*.

Those who meditate on a mantra regularly and sincerely find the eternal friend, the mantra, during this time
of transition. A meditator cannot be lonely and insecure
during the time of death because he or she is accompanied by the mantra. The mantra is the leader that guides
you from this world to the next and this realization comes
at least a moment before death actually occurs. Thus a dying
meditator attains freedom from fear, insecurity, and loneliness in this very lifetime, and departs from this platform
gracefully.

Seeker: I was born and raised in a culture in which I was not exposed to meditation or any form of spiritual discipline. I am willing to do things that are good for my health and that increase my inner peace as long as such practices do not disturb my religious faith. The kind of meditation and spiritual discipline you are talking about seems to be more fruitful and easier if I have the right background—that is, a good grasp of yoga philosophy. Is it too late for me to prepare myself to advance on the spiritual path?

Swamiji: It doesn't matter where you were born, or which denomination you belong to. As long as you realize the importance of having a healthy body and a balanced mind, you can start practicing those things which make sense to you. You don't have to abandon your faith or embrace any other one. Stay wherever you are. Do not disturb your family or your society.

Practice truth in thought, speech, and action. Love for truth will help you understand what your most urgent problems and concerns are. Soon you will notice that you are not interested in either hell or heaven—you simply want to be happy and peaceful. Your former interest in hell and heaven was not yours; it was superimposed on you by others who exploited your tendencies toward fear and greed.

In the initial stages of your inward journey, you begin to work with your body. The body is a tool for achieving both worldly and spiritual wealth. You should practice exercises that make your body healthy whether you are Christian, Hindu, Muslim, Jewish, or Buddhist. Similarly, breathing exercises do not conflict with any religion.

You also need a system of gathering the power of your senses and withdrawing them from the external world. You must learn how to relax and provide maximum rest for your body, senses, and nervous system so that your mind is free from the complaints of your body. This process

of withdrawing the senses from the external world and re-
laxing does not require you to be born in any particular
religious or cultural background.

Then comes the method of concentration. At this stage
of your inward journey, choose an object on which to focus your mind and make sure that this object is intrinsi-
cally peaceful and carries the least amount of sectarian
baggage. Improve your concentration and one-pointedness
by constantly focusing your mind on one chosen object. This
is a process of retraining your mind.

Ordinarily the mind has a habit of running from one
object to another. This roving tendency drains an enormous
amount of energy, causing weakness and frustration. No
one with a scattered mind can expect to be successful in
either the external world or in the spiritual world. Practicing a method of concentration enables you to cultivate
one-pointedness. With the help of a one-pointed mind you
can resolve even the most complicated issues. You can
penetrate the greatest of all mysteries. You need a purified, one-pointed, and disciplined mind to unveil the truth
that saints from different traditions share with us. A person with a healthy body and one-pointed mind can practice Christianity, Judaism, Hinduism, Islam, or Buddhism
much more accurately and successfully than can those
who are unhealthy and confused.

According to the sages of the Himalayas, the best spiritual discipline is the one that helps you gather the means
and resources for undertaking a spiritual practice. That is
why they designed a holistic lifestyle, which in ancient
times was called *raja yoga*. Simple principles of life—such
as practicing non-violence, truthfulness, non-stealing,
moderation in sense activity, non-possessiveness, cleanliness, contentment, tapas (disciplining the body, mind, and
senses), the study of genuine scriptures, and faith in a
higher truth—are the foundation of holistic living. There
are no religious, ethical, moral, or social schools in the

world that do not honor these ten principles.

With the help of this simple practice of spirituality—which consists of these ten principles, physical exercise, breathing exercises, relaxation, concentration, and meditation—you automatically begin to overcome your doubt and skepticism. You know what you are doing and you know that it's helping you. You will notice that your understanding of your religious faith, your family life, and your relationships have improved. You become a more tolerant and loving human being. That is a great achievement in itself.

Afterwards your mind and heart will tell you what should follow next. This process of gradual transformation and unfoldment is healthy and long-lasting. Depending on your degree of emotional maturity and intellectual understanding, you will aspire to find a spiritual path that is perfect for you. There are many jackets in the market that are attractive and well-made, but the best one is one that fits you. This is also the case with a spiritual path and spiritual disciplines. All lead to the same goal but the best path is the one that suits you. These man-made, cultural and religious backgrounds need to follow the truth, not the other way around.

10

Putting the Teachings in Perspective

Although it may seem, after reading the foregoing chapters, that the teachings of the sages are diverse, they can
be summarized in one phrase: "The truth is One; its faces
are many." In the beginning and intermediate stages of
spiritual unfoldment, the sages may have had different experiences but once they transcended the boundaries of time,
space, and causation and reached the highest state of
samadhi, they all attained the experience of unitary consciousness. As the ultimate truth revealed itself in its brilliance and perfection, the sages experienced the oneness
of the microcosm and the macrocosm and came to know
that that which lies outside us also exists inside us. After
this experience the knowledge of life here and hereafter—
the knowledge of manifest and unmanifest reality—was no
longer a mystery.

However it was impossible for the sages to communicate this experience to those whose consciousness was still
confined by apparent reality. They had to find a way to

bridge the gulf between their realization of unitary consciousness and the consciousness of ordinary humans. They communicated only that part of their experience that could be understood and appreciated by those living in a specific place at a specific time. To do this they employed the language, symbols, and idioms that were in use at the time they were teaching. Thus the differences in their teachings are rooted, not in differences in their ultimate experiences, but in how much of that experience they were able to share with their students and the idiom in which they communicated it. These differences in presentation aside, all sages speak with one voice when describing the method of inner unfoldment: "Be practical!"

Their teachings emphasize the importance of finding out where you are in your personal evolution, what your pressing needs are, what your resources are, and how much freedom you have to do what you want to do. They all knew that the only way to minimize obstacles is to make an accurate assessment of your current situation. Once you have done this, you must follow a systematic path to reach your goal. There are several key points to consider before embarking on the path of spiritual unfoldment. They are explained briefly below.

Look at the Broad Picture of Life

The life of an individual is like an iceberg floating in the ocean of cosmic existence. Only a small portion of it is visible at any given time. The same is true of life. We become frustrated, disappointed, and depressed because we identify ourselves with the trivial matters of day-to-day life. This can make us feel hopeless. Every single pleasure and pain, success and failure, loss and gain affects us. We are tossed about by experiences which are not particularly significant in the larger scheme of things.

Like little children we are happy one moment, cranky the next. We forget that birth, death, and all the experiences in between are just a ripple in the eternal stream of life. Out of ignorance, we place too much importance on these momentary experiences, forgetting that life has a higher purpose. In the depths of our hearts, however, we want to reach the place where we are free from the cycle of birth and death; we know that the greatest loss is to fail to reach that place before the body returns to dust.

In the deepest part of our being, we know that true happiness comes only from the realization that we are free. However at the surface level, we busy ourselves with trivial concerns, even though we know that such activities will not help in the long run. There is a chasm between what we know in our hearts and what we are driven to do at the surface level.

We live in two different worlds with no way of bridging the gulf between them. While living in the outer world, we forget about our spiritual goals. When we remember them, we condemn ourselves for this forgetfulness. While attempting to live in our inner world, we find ourselves distracted by worldly concerns. The failure to keep the company of our best friend, the inner soul, creates a sense of loneliness and "missingness," which is the source of our misery.

The scriptures describe two major paths for overcoming this problem and attaining happiness: *pravritti marga* and *nivritti marga*. Pravritti marga requires keeping ourselves active in the world while performing only those actions that neutralize, or at least minimize, the effects of previous karmic bonds. On this path we must make sure that our actions are not motivated by selfish desires. That's very difficult.

Nivritti marga requires renouncing the world and all worldly concerns. Without getting involved in what goes on in the external world, we must remain focused only on our inner Self. This renunciation also includes renunciation of our desires, attachments, memories of the past, and anxieties about the future. That's very difficult too.

Between these two paths lies a third—the path of balance and integration known as *raja yoga*, the royal path. This path is so broad and all-embracing that we can all follow it at our own pace, in spite of having different capacities and backgrounds. This path lies between getting lost in the world and running away from it. The aspirant practices living in the world while remaining above it. Performing your duties skillfully and lovingly, without clinging to the fruit of your actions, is the key. However, before you dedicate yourself to this path, it is of utmost importance to know which part of your life needs immediate attention.

Start from Where You Are

Before embarking on any journey, it is important to be familiar with the map of your route and to know exactly where you are on that map. How successful you are at reaching the nearest highway depends on how familiar you are with the locality in which you live and the surrounding terrain. With regard to your spiritual journey, this means knowing your temperament, your habit patterns, and your principal strengths and weaknesses before committing yourself to a particular spiritual practice. Scrutinize the part of your life that troubles you the most. You will not be able to escape all your problems. Resolving such troubles is as important as actually undertaking a spiritual practice. The fatigue brought on by your job and anxiety over unpaid bills are examples of problems that will have to be resolved.

Such problems are usually the result of a failure to fulfill your worldly duties and obligations. There are no spiritual practices for resolving these problems and you will not have the freedom of mind to attend to your spiritual practice until you have resolved them. One of the biggest mistakes that aspirants make is to commit themselves to spiritual practice as a means of escaping from their duties. If you shun your duties, you will commit yourself to the practices at a level you cannot sustain, which will be counterproductive in the long run.

Another aspect of starting from where you are is to become acquainted with your physical capacity. According to the scriptures, "The body is the basic instrument for the process of spiritual development." Physical vitality is the key to progressing on the path. Begin by working within the limits of your current capacity and then gradually work toward expanding that capacity. Physical pain, disease, and occasional illness are facts of life. They cannot be ignored or dissolved by mere philosophy. You must design your practice so that it does not aggravate your physical problems and so that your physical problems do not disturb your practice.

Choose a Path

Analyze your temperament and habits to determine your proclivities. Such an analysis will enable you to choose a specific aspect of raja yoga as your main focus.

If you are an intellectual, then *jnana yoga*—the path of knowledge—will be the most effective. If you are emotional, you can transform your emotions into love and devotion and attain union with God by following the path of *bhakti*. If you are healthy and have little interest in studying scriptures, sharpening your intellect, or purifying your emotions, then the path of *hatha yoga*, under the guidance of a competent yogi, will be the most fruitful. The path of *karma yoga*—the yoga of selfless action—is suitable if you enjoy doing things for others and sharing the fruits of your actions. If your main interest lies in knowing yourself at every level and awakening the infinite, dormant forces within you, then follow the path of *kundalini yoga*.

Regardless of which path you choose, you must begin with a healthy body and a sound mind. If you have a variety of beautifully tailored jackets, but are so ill or in such a bad mood that you can't leave your bedroom, these jackets are useless. Similarly if you know a great deal about spiritual practices and have been given a number of practices by competent teachers, but have pain in your knees or are distracted by memories and hopes each time you sit to meditate, then these practices will have very little effect. Keeping your body and mind in good health requires following a routine of proper exercise, breathing practices, relaxation, and a systematic process of meditation. The following basic guidelines fall into four categories: physical exercises, breathing exercises, relaxation exercises, and meditation.

Physical Exercise

According to yoga science, the best exercises are those that stimulate the whole body rather than just one particular muscle group. Yoga postures stretch and stimulate the muscles, ligaments, and joints, restoring elasticity and tone to the body. They stimulate circulation and revitalize the internal organs, brain, and nervous system. Practicing these postures enables the respiratory system to perform more efficiently by taking in greater amounts of oxygen and eliminating more toxins. The postures also increase resistance to fatigue and relieve tension. A session of yogic exercises is designed so that exertion on limbs or organs is balanced with rest and relaxation.

Yoga postures are not a substitute for aerobic exercise; even during peak performance, these exercises don't interfere with the normal functioning of the lungs and heart. The effectiveness of yogic exercises lies in the coordination of breath and movement. Yogic postures can be practiced by the strong and the weak, the healthy and the relatively unhealthy. These postures are designed to create and maintain a healthy body and a peaceful mind. There are four key points to remember:

1. Coordinate breath and movements. With each movement, pay attention to your breath; make sure that your

physical movement does not interfere with your breathing pattern and vice versa. Inhale each time your chest expands and exhale when it contracts.

2. Stay within your capacity. Be aware of your current level of strength, flexibility, and stamina. Stop before you feel fatigued. The object is to feel good—both while you are exercising and after you are finished.

3. Balance your routine. The stress on a particular limb, organ, or muscle group created by one exercise should be counterbalanced by another exercise. For example the plough posture stretches the back of the neck and should be followed by the fish posture, which stretches the front of the neck.

4. Relax. Begin and end each exercise session with a systematic relaxation.

How Much and When to Exercise

Yogic exercises work with the entire body, especially the internal organs. The effects are subtle so be careful not to do too much. It's best to start with 20 to 30 minutes of simple *asanas* and watch how your body responds as you include more advanced postures in your routine. Maintaining a regular, moderate practice and following it with a period of relaxation will enable you to improve your capacity in a delightful and amazing way. How your body feels and your sense of enjoyment are the best indications of how much to exercise.

Traditionally morning is considered to be the best time for yogic exercise because the stomach is empty, the colon is clean, and the atmosphere is calm and soothing. However in the modern world, evening may be better for two reasons: (1) Because of stress and lack of proper rest, many people are stiff in the morning; and (2) Many people are too busy in the morning for a relaxed session.

The main drawback to evening practice is that people are tired or jangled after a hectic day (or too full because they stopped off at the local carry-out on the way home from work). If you choose to practice in the evening, then make time for yourself by cutting down on evening commitments. Be sure to do a relaxation exercise to eliminate tension and fatigue before starting yoga exercises.

Breathing Exercises

The scriptures say that "breath is life and life is breath." Breath is the link between the individual and the cosmic being and between the body and mind. Through the breath, the individual receives vitality from the atmosphere and remains connected with cosmic awareness. A healthy breathing pattern ensures the health of both body and mind. The yogic breathing techniques are called *pranayama*, which literally means expanding the vital force or gaining control over the activities of the vital force within. The following three breathing techniques are especially suitable for us "modern" people: diaphragmatic breathing, channel purification, and two-to-one breathing.

Diaphragmatic Breathing

The diaphragm is the muscle that divides the torso into two separate chambers, the thorax and the abdomen. It forms the floor of the thorax and rests against the base of the lungs. As it relaxes during exhalation, this dome-shaped muscle presses against the lungs from below. Inhalation follows as the diaphragm contracts. In a healthy person, the movement of the diaphragm is responsible for 75 percent of the exchange of gases in the lungs. However, the diaphragm is often tense, blocking natural breathing, and causing fatigue, tension, and more serious problems.

One of the first aims of yoga is to re-establish good breathing habits as a means of improving both physical and mental health. Restoring the habit of diaphragmatic breathing accomplishes this effectively.

You can learn what diaphragmatic breathing feels like

by lying in the crocodile posture. To assume the crocodile, lie on your stomach with your legs a comfortable distance apart. The toes can be pointed in or out, whichever is more comfortable. Fold the arms in front of the body, resting the hands on the biceps. Position the arms so that the base of the rib cage touches the floor, as pictured.

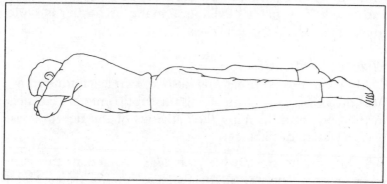

The Crocodile Pose

As you breathe in this position, the diaphragm moves vertically, pressing against the lungs from below. When you inhale, the abdomen expands, pressing against the floor and the back gently rises. As you exhale the abdomen contracts, and the back gently falls. Both these effects are produced by the movement of the diaphragm.

Establish the habit of diaphragmatic breathing in daily life, 24 hours a day. You can do this by practicing the crocodile pose two times a day for five to ten minutes. When you're finished, roll onto your back and observe your abdomen as it expands and contracts with the breath. Next, sit in a chair and again watch your breathing, keeping your abdomen relaxed. The last step is to stand as you continue to breathe diaphragmatically. Practice regularly until diaphragmatic breathing becomes a habit.

The following checklist will help you to evaluate your breathing:

1. The breath flows smoothly.

2. There is no pause between breaths.
3. The breath flows silently.
4. Exhalation and inhalation are approximately equal.
5. The breath is deep, yet the upper chest barely moves.

Diaphragmatic breathing enables you to feel your best, gain emotional control and balance, and reduce fatigue and stress. The habit of diaphragmatic breathing is basic to all yogic breathing practices.

Channel Purification

Alternate nostril breathing, also known as channel purification, is a means of purifying the subtle energy channels in the body and bringing the activities of the nervous system to a state of balance.

1. Sit on the floor with your legs crossed in the easy pose or on a chair with the feet flat on the floor. Make sure the head, neck, and trunk are aligned.

2. Bring the right hand to the nose, folding the index finger and the middle finger so that the right thumb can be used to close the right nostril and the ring finger can be used to close the left nostril.

3. Close the left nostril and exhale completely through the right nostril.

4. At the end of the exhalation, close the right nostril and inhale through the left nostril slowly and completely. The inhalation and exhalation should be of equal duration.

5. Repeat this cycle of exhalation with the right nostril and inhalation with the left nostril two more times.

6. At the end of the third inhalation through the **left** nostril, exhale completely through the **left** nostril, keeping the right nostril closed with the thumb.

7. At the end of the exhalation, close the left nostril and inhale through the right nostril.

8. Repeat two more times, exhaling through the left nostril and inhaling through the right nostril.

9. In summary:

EXHALE	INHALE
Right	Left
Right	Left
Right	Left
Left	Right
Left	Right
Left	Right

This cycle can be repeated three times. Make sure you do an equal number of inhalations and exhalations through each nostril. Gradually lengthen the duration of the inhalation and the exhalation with practice.

Two-to-One Breathing

This particular breathing practice is an absolute necessity for people living in cities where the air is polluted because it cleans the lungs and purifies the blood. The method is as follows:

1. First establish a pattern of even breathing (inhalation and exhalation are of equal duration). You may do this practice either in the corpse pose or in a sitting posture. You can count to make sure that the length of your inhalation and exhalation are equal.

2. After you have established a pattern of even breathing (it may take a few days or a couple of weeks), resolve to exhale longer than you inhale. You can accomplish this by counting to four while inhaling, for example, and to eight while exhaling. As your practice continues, periodically try adding a few more counts to your exhalation and see how comfortable you feel. Set a goal that within two or three months, you will count to ten while inhaling and to twenty while exhaling. When you have accomplished this, stay at this level for a while.

3. Later on, try to expand the duration of your inhalation, always keeping the exhalation twice as long as the

inhalation. For example if you inhale for 12 counts, then you must exhale for 24 counts. If you inhale for 15 counts, then you must exhale for 30 counts. A 15:30 ratio of inhalation to exhalation is excellent.

Relaxation Exercises

The word "relaxation" may be somewhat misleading. If you *try* to relax, you are bound to fail. Relaxation must be learned systematically and then allowed to progress naturally. In relaxation one learns the art of letting go.

There are many methods of yoga relaxation. The following exercise forms the base from which many succeeding exercises may be learned. It is effective in relieving tension and helps to bring the mind into a state of relaxed concentration.

Lie on your back. Use a thin cushion under the head. Cover your body with a sheet or thin shawl and place the legs a comfortable distance apart. The arms are slightly separated from the body and the palms are turned up. The spine should not be bent to either side. Take time to adjust your posture and then become still. Close your eyes and be aware of the presence of your body, the space around you, and the place where your body rests. Observe your entire body from head to toe. Cultivate and enjoy the perfect stillness of your body.

Now bring your attention to your breath. Observe each exhalation and inhalation and let the breath become deep and diaphragmatic. Breathing out, release all tension, waste, fatigue, and worry. Inhale a feeling of energy and well-being. Do not pause between the breaths. Repeat this a few times. Next, gently survey your body mentally. You will naturally release tension in the places where you observe it. This process of "letting go" is the relaxation process. Proceed from the head to the toes and then back to the head, following this sequence:

> forehead
> eyebrows and eyes

nose*
cheeks
mouth
jaw
chin
neck
shoulders
upper arms
lower arms
hands
fingers
fingertips*
fingers
hands
lower arms
upper arms
shoulders
chest
heart center**
stomach
navel region
pelvic region
upper legs
lower legs
feet
toes**

At these places, you may pause for two or four** relaxed breaths when you are traveling from head to toe.

Now reverse the order and proceed upward, this time without any pauses.

Some practice will be required to complete this exercise without lapse of attention. If your mind wanders, simply and gently bring it back to the relaxation process.

After progressing through the whole body, gently relax your mind. Turn your attention to the quiet flow of your breath. For a few minutes, rest and feel that this subtle stream of breath is a link joining you to the cosmos. You will be in harmony and at peace. Then roll onto your side and sit up.

Meditation

Use relaxation techniques and alternate nostril breathing to overcome fatigue before sitting for meditation. Make a mental resolution that for the next 20 to 30 minutes you will entertain neither memories of the past nor thoughts about the future.

1. Sit cross-legged, either on the floor or on a chair with your feet flat on the floor. Make sure that your head, neck, and trunk are aligned. Relax your shoulders and let your hands rest on your knees, thighs, or legs.

2. Breathe gently and naturally without jerks, pauses, or noise.

3. Focus on your breath and watch how it flows from the tip of your nostrils to your heart center as you exhale, and from the heart center to the tip of your nostrils as you inhale.

4. After a few breaths, focus mentally on the sound "so hum." While you inhale, listen to the sound "so" and while you exhale, listen to the sound "hum." Let your mind, breath, and the sound "so hum" flow together. Stay with this practice as long as you find it enjoyable.

Those who have received a personal mantra through formal initiation may focus on that mantra. If you have received mantra initiation, follow the meditation instructions given to you. The instructions you receive personally supersede these general guidelines.

The Real Journey

Practicing yogic exercises, breathing techniques, relaxation, and concentration on the breath will prepare you for the spiritual journey. After you have been practicing these techniques for awhile, you'll notice that, to a great degree, your body and mind will follow your instructions. The smooth and rhythmic flow of your breath will have helped you eliminate many obstacles. You will have a sense that a great joy lies deep within you, but so far you have not attained it. For this you need more direct and personalized guidance.

In the beginning, meditating on the sound "so hum" is rewarding, but after a while you will reach a plateau. That is the time to look for more personal guidance. An experienced teacher can help you to understand the exact nature of your personal *sadhana*. A good teacher knows how to introduce you to the teacher within so that you can keep receiving guidance without relying overtly on external teaching.

An authentic teacher will introduce you to the divine by initiating you into a mantra, the divine word that in the beginning of creation was with God and was God. In Sanskrit literature it is called "mantra"; in other spiritual literature, it is called "nam". In the Judeo-Christian tradition it is called "the Word."

A teacher gives precise instruction in how to string this arrow of the mantra on the bow of the mind, letting the arrow fly at the moment that your entire awareness is focused on the target. As it penetrates the target, a multileveled mystery is unveiled. The purpose of life is accomplished only after this occurs. Fear of the unknown vanishes and you are truly at peace. True knowledge dawns and in the light of that knowledge, neither present actions nor the actions of the past bind you anymore. Such a person is *jivanmukta*—liberated here and now.

Because the highest duty—Self-realization—has been accomplished, a jivanmukta is free from all duties. However such enlightened souls cannot become inactive. The eternal dance of the benign and beautiful divine force that they experience within manifests in their thought, speech, and action. The body and mind of these adepts move spontaneously to perform actions for the benefit of their fellow beings. From an enlightened person's perspective, the actions they perform are virtually effortless because those actions are motivated and carried out by the will of the divine.

Even when they withdraw themselves from the world and live in seclusion, they continue doing their sadhana, not because they have something yet to achieve but because they find delight in doing so. To keep discovering the subtle laws of the forces that control the manifest world is their recreation. They practice and gain knowledge of highly evolved spiritual sciences, such as *pranavidya*, the science of prana; *daharavidya*, the science of the internal cave; *suryavijnana*, the science of the mystical sun; *shrividya*, the highest of all spiritual sciences; and so on.

From our perspective, practicing spirituality seems to be hard work. It requires taking care of our bodies, disciplining our senses (which they don't like), inducing the mind to turn inward (which it has forgotten how to do), and finally placing top priority on the knowledge of the soul. We pay a high price too—we have to let go of the past to live in the present and rid ourselves of worldly trash to enjoy the fragrance of the divine Self. But once we have accomplished that much, the journey seems to become effortless. Working hard—doing our practices sincerely—is the way to prepare ourselves but finally it's the enlightened ones—the *brahma rishis*—who pull us up and place us on the highest summit.

As Sri Swami Rama tells us: "Then the illumined practitioner sits calm in his celestial sessions with the highest of powers and drinks the wine of infinite beatitude. This child of immortality is a child of universal parents, protected all the time by the Mother Divine. This rapturous child of bliss, intoxicated in delight, remains one with the divine. He becomes a sage, a sleepless envoy and ever-wakeful guide for those who tread the path. Such a leader on the path marches in front of human people, to comfort, help, and enlighten them."

Glossary

ABHASA VADA. Reflectionism; a philosophical doctrine according to which the material world is simply a reflection of what lies in the realm of pure consciousness. According to this theory, the absolute reality alone exists—the external world is mere appearance.

ABHYASA. Practice; a yogic term that refers to the process of making an effort to stay on one point, i.e., the object of meditation. Accomplishment in the practice is attained when one continues practicing for a long period of time without interruption.

ACHARAH. Healthy living; a code of conduct comprised of guidelines for healthy living.

ACHARYA. One whose example can be confidently followed in all areas of life; a teacher who has authority in a particular area of learning; a person well-versed in spiritual texts; a spiritual teacher.

ADVAITA. Non-dual transcendental truth. According to Vedanta philosophy, behind all diversities there lies only one truth called Brahman. It is due to ignorance that one sees duality, but as knowledge dawns, duality disappears and the aspirant realizes his or her oneness with the absolute truth.

ADVAITA BHAKTI. The expression of divine love where the lover and the beloved have become one; the state of ectasy in which the devotee is completely merged in, and has become one with, the divine.

ADVAITA VEDANTA. Non-dualistic school of Vedanta philosophy. There are several sub-schools of Vedanta such as *dvaita* which expounds dualism; *vishista advaita*, which expounds qualified non-dualism, and so forth. *Advaita vedanta*, taught by the sages of the Upanishads, is the most prominent of the Vedanta schools.

AGHORA MARGA. One of the most esoteric spiritual paths. Literally *a* means "not," and *ghora* means "violent, destructive." This path leads to the realization of *aghora shakti*, the most benevolent and benign form of the divine force.

213

AGNI VIDYA. The esoteric science of fire.

AHARA SHUDDHI. Purification of food. According to the scriptures, not only the body but also our thinking process is greatly affected by the food we eat. Therefore, eating pure, fresh, nutritious, and light food in right amounts, at the right time, with the right mental attitude is of utmost importance. Without observing a dietary discipline, one cannot successfully work with oneself.

AHIMSA. Non-violence; non-hurting; non-killing; the first and foremost among five restraints (*yamas*) mentioned in yoga literature.

ANANDAMAYA KOSHA. The blissful sheath. According to yoga philosophy, a human being is comprised of several sheaths or layers: the physical sheath, energy sheath, mental sheath, sheath of knowledge, and sheath of bliss. The sheath theory is used as a model to study ourselves systematically and penetrate our inner being, layer by layer, and ultimately reach beyond all sheaths to the *Atman*, pure consciousness, which is completely free and pure.

APARA BHAKTI. See *bhakti*.

APARA VIDYA. See *vidya*.

APARIGHRAHA. Non-possessiveness; one of the five *maha-vratas*, the great vows.

ASANA. Literally, the place to sit or the seat on which a sadhaka sits; the meditative pose, the practice of postures.

ASHVAMEDHA. The horse sacrifice. In the Upanishads, it refers to the spiritual discipline in which one systematically learns how to tame the senses (the horses) and offer them to the fire of Brahman.

ATMA KRIPA. See *kripa*.

ATMA SHAKTI. The power of Atman; inner strength; also identified with *kundalini shakti*.

ATMAN. The pure Self; pure consciousness. The Atman is the real Self, as opposed to ego, which identifies itself with the objects of the world.

AVADHOOTA. One whose *vasanas* and *samskaras* have been completely washed off; an enlightened being who, due to her or his transcendence of the mundane level of awareness remains oblivious to worldly norms.

AVIDYA. Ignorance; lack of knowledge; mistaking one thing for something else; the primeval affliction—the mother of all other afflictions such as ego, attachment, aversion, and fear. It is overcome only by *vidya*—true knowledge, or the knowledge of the Self.

BABA. An affectionate term for an elderly person; a term used for *sadhus*, swamis, and wandering saints.

BHAIRAVA. Synonymous with Shiva.

BHAKTI. Devotion; love; refers to unconditional love for the divine. True love and devotion for the highest truth alone can uplift the consciousness of the aspirant. Through intense love and devotion for the divine, an aspirant can attain the unitary experience, a state of highest delight. Therefore, *bhakti yoga* is considered to be an independent path of spirituality. There are two levels of the experience of bhakti—*apara bhakti* and *para bhakti*.

Apara bhakti is the lower stage of bhakti, in which an aspirant feels that he or she is separate from the Beloved (God), and makes an effort to express love and devotion, by actions such as singing the glory of God, chanting, worshipping, and so forth.

However when one becomes constantly aware of the presence of God, when every single thought, speech, and action is fully mingled with the awareness of God and an aspirant experiences unity with God, such a state is *para bhakti*—the highest state of bhakti. *Apara bhakti* refers to the process of loving God, whereas *para bhakti* refers to the state of awareness in which the adept simply remains inebriated in divine love.

BRAHMACHARI. One who dwells in Brahman consciousness; one who practices continence; one who is totally dedicated to the study of the Vedas and is not involved in secular, family life.

BRAHMAN. All pervading, eternal, and absolute truth.

BRAHMA NADI. The most subtle *nadi*, which transcends even *sushumna*. It is through this *nadi* that a yogi goes beyond the *ajna chakra* and attains a particular state of *samadhi* called *unmani*, the state beyond mind.

BRAHMANA. A particular portion of Vedic literature dedicated to rituals and ceremonies.

BRAHMA-RANDHRA. Literally, the hole of Brahman or the passage leading to Brahman; a particular *nadi*, also known as *brahma nadi*, situated between the *ajna chakra* and the *sahasrara chakra*.

BRAHMA RISHI. The knower of Brahman; a seer; a realized soul.

BUDDHI. The intellect; the faculty of reason and discernment.

CHANDRA VIDYA. Lunar science; the science of the mystical moon; also known as *soma vidya*. The first reference to this science is found in the tenth book of the Rig Veda, and is later elaborated in the Upanishads and tantric texts.

CHITTA. Mind; mind field. A generic term referring to all faculties of mind, such as *manas*, the lower mind; *ahamkara*, ego; and *buddhi*, intellect. In some cases, *chitta* refers to the unconscious mind.

DAHARAVIDYA. The spiritual science that leads to the realization of the pure space of consciousness.

DAMA. Self-restraint; self-control; self-mastery; discipline of senses.

DANDA. A staff that a renunciate carries all the time.

DARSHANA. Vision; direct realization as opposed to the information gained through the senses. This word is used in three ways: (1) To have a glance of a holy person or an image of a deity residing at the shrine or in the temple; (2) An extraordinary vision of imperceptible divine beings; and (3) A system of philosophy that holds revelation in high regard, as opposed to relying exclusively on intellectual speculation.

DASHANAMI. In addition to five main monastic orders established by Shankaracharya, there are ten more renunciate traditions called *dashanami*.

DEHA VIJNANA. The yogic science pertaining to deeper understanding of the human body and the subtle forces that regulate the functions of the body. This science deals not only with the physical structure of the body, such as muscular, skeletal, and neurological systems, but also with the *pranic* forces and the intricate *nadi* system.

DEVADASI. A woman servant of god; a particular community of women who totally dedicated their lives in service of the temples, mainly in south India, earning their living by giving dance performances at the temples. This practice degenerated into a form of involuntary servitude and was banned after India gained her independence in 1947.

DHARMA. Duty; spiritual and ethical disciplines that are helpful for the growth of an individual as well as society.

DHUNI. The fire yogis prepare and constantly attend as part of their spiritual discipline.

DIVYA CHAKSU. The divine eye; the intuitive eye.

GAYATRI MANTRA. One of the best known mantras from the Yajur Veda; its name comes from the meter in which it is written.

GAYATRI PURASCHARANA. A systematic practice of meditating on the *gayatri mantra* in a specific period of time.

GAYATRI SHAKTI. The *shakti* of the *gayatri mantra*; also known as *Savitri*.

GOLOKA DHAMA. The realm of eternity and immortality that is attained only by perfectly accomplished yogis. It is this particular realm of existence where mystical cows with seven horns, the mystical sun with seven rays, the mystical fire with its seven tongues of flame, and the intuitive wisdom (*prajna*) with its seven levels of revelation ever shine. This is also the eternal *loka* of Vishnu, the all-pervading, omniscient, eternal being.

GUNAS. The intrinsic forces of primordial nature, namely *sattva*, *rajas*, and *tamas*.

GURUBHAI. A spiritual brother; someone studying with the same master.

GURUDEVA. A way of referring to the guru or spiritual master with honor and respect.

GURU KRIPA. See *kripa*.

HANSA. Swan; it refers to accomplished yogis who live in the Himalayas, around and beyond Gangotri.

HATHA YOGA. The path of yoga consisting of the first four rungs of raja yoga: *yama*, *niyama*, *asana*, and *pranayama*.

HIMA-SAMADHI. Casting off one's body in deep snow.

ICCHA SHAKTI. Power of will; the primordial will of the divine, the intrinsic power of consciousness; the creative power, followed by the power of knowledge and the power of action. The most profound study of *iccha shakti* is found in shaivist and shrividya schools of philosophy.

ISHTA DEVATA. The chosen name and form of the Godhead.

ISHWARA KRIPA. See *kripa.*

JALA-SAMADHI. Casting off one's body in water.

JALEBI. An Indian sweet.

JNANA YOGA. The yoga of knowledge. According to this school, it is through knowledge that one attains liberation, burns *samskaras* (the subtle impressions of all past deeds), and becomes free once and for all.

JNANI. The knower of truth; one who has knowledge.

JIVA. The individual self; the consciousness that identifies with body, senses, and mind, and as a result becomes a victim of pleasure and pain, birth and death.

JIVANMUKTA. One who is liberated here and now; one who, due to an elevated state of knowledge, remains unaffected by the charms and temptations of the world and the pairs of opposites—pleasure and pain, loss and gain, success and failure.

JNANI. One who has attained knowledge.

KAMA. Desire; an intrinsic aspect of divine will; the first step of the descent of consciousness toward manifestation of the material world.

KAMA KOLA. Primordial desire, the power of will *(iccha shakti)*; in *tantra shastra* it refers to the triangle and the forces symbolized by the triangle.

KAMANDALU. Water vessel; traditional water pot that sadhus carry.

KARUNA. Compassion.

KRIPA. Grace; a favor; divine help. According to the yogic texts, the most subtle hurdles are removed by divine grace, which usually descends after the aspirant has made the utmost effort. The full advantage of this divine grace is achieved when the four-fold "graces" meet. They are: *shastra kripa*, the grace of the scriptures; *atma kripa*, the grace of one's Self; *guru kripa*, the grace of the guru; and *Ishwara kripa*, the grace of God.

KUNDALINI YOGA. The path of yoga where one finds a systematic method of awakening the dormant force and leading it step by step to the *sahasrara*, the highest center of consciousness.

LAKSHMANA REKHA. The line drawn by Lakshmana, the younger brother of Rama, the hero of the Ramayana. Thus, it is a line of demarcation that is supposedly charged with a protective spiritual energy, so that an aspirant doing *sadhana* inside the boundary remains free of all obstacles that originate outside the line.

LILA. Divine play; the play of the divine force that manifests in the form of creation, maintenance, and annihilation of the universe.

MAHA MAYA. The highest creative force; the intrinsic power of of Brahman or Parama-shiva.

MAHA PURASCHARNA. A grand spiritual undertaking; in the case of meditation on the *gayatri mantra*, a maha purascharna would consist of repeating the mantra 2,100,000 times within a defined period of time—16 months or 32 months, for example. Strict disciplines related to diet, silence, refraining from socializing, sleeping moderately, and so forth, go along with this practice.

MAHAVIDYA(S). The great knowledge, or the great spiritual paths. In the yoga tradition of *shakti sadhana*, there are ten main esoteric paths, all expounding a highly specialized method of meditation on shakti. Those ten paths are known as the *mahavidyas*. They are Kali, Tara, Chhinnamasta, Sodashi (Srividya), Matangi, Tripura-bhairavi, Bhuvaneshvari, Bagalamukhi, Kamala, and Dhumavati.

MANANA. Pondering; contemplating.

MANDALA. The depiction of the personified form of a mantra; a visible depiction of the invisible forces of nature, as well as different aspects of the human psyche. A thorough knowledge of myths and symbols is necessary to grasp the essence of a mandala.

MAYA. The creative force of Brahman.

MIMAMSA. System of philosophy that evolved from the Vedas and emphasizes a ritualistic approach to spirituality.

MUMUKSHA. Desire for liberation. One of the qualities a student of *jnana yoga* must cultivate before the study of the scriptures and contemplation can become a means to spiritual unfoldment.

NADA. The eternal sound yogis hear during meditation.

NARAYANA. The primordial master; the spiritual guide of all previous teachers; the sage from whom the spiritual wisdom flows forever.

NIDIDHYASANA. Applying knowledge that one has gained from the study and deep contemplation of the scriptures.

NIVRITTI MARGA. Detaching oneself from worldly involvement; the path of renunciation as opposed to the path of a householder.

PANDIT. A learned person; a Sanskrit scholar; one who has access to ancient scriptures. Ideally, a pandit is one whose actions are not motivated by personal whims and who has burnt the seeds of all karmas in the fire of knowledge.

PARA BHAKTI. See *bhakti.*

PARA VIDYA. The highest knowledge. For details, see *vidya.*

PARAKAYA PRAVESHA. An advanced technique of yoga that enables a yogi to cast off the body at will and acquire another body as he or she chooses.

PARAMAHANSA. An accomplished yogi, who is able to discern the real from the unreal and remains unattached to worldly objects, including her or his own body and senses.

PARIVRAJAKA. A monk who has no permanent residence, possesses nothing, and continually travels from place to place.

PITHAM. A spiritual center; a seat of spiritual learning.

PRAKRITI. The primordial cause of the universe; nature.

PRANA. The life force.

PRANAVIDYA. The science of *prana*, the vital force.

PRANAYAMA. Control over and expansion of the vital force; breathing exercises.

PRATIBIMBA VADA. Reflectionism; see *abhasa vada.*

PRATYAHARA. Withdrawal of the senses; the fifth rung in the eight-rung ladder of *raja yoga.*

PRAVRITTI MARGA. the path of a householder as opposed to the path of a renunciate.

PURNA PATRA. A container or bowl that is always filled with food.

RAJA YOGA. The royal path; the path of yoga in which the entire practice is described in eight steps: *yama, niyama, asana, pranayama, pratyahara, dharana, dhyana,* and *samadhi.*

RAJAS. One of the attributes of nature; the power of activity.

RISHI. The seer; a sage to whom a mantra or a group of mantras is revealed.

SADGURU. A genuine spiritual master, as opposed to the teachers from whom one gathers information on diverse subjects; a spiritual master capable of purifying a student's heart and opening the spiritual eye.

SADHAKA. A spiritual aspirant; a seeker.

SADHANA. Spiritual practice.

SADHU. Saint; one who has dedicated her or his life to spiritual pursuit.

SAMADHANA. Putting together or arranging in proper order; putting the teachings of different teachers and scriptures in proper context.

SAMADHI. State of tranquillity; state of mind where there are no thought constructs.

SAMAYA. One of the three stages or schools of *tantra yoga;* see *tantra.*

SAMKALPA. Determination.

SAMKALPA SHAKTI. The power of determination.

SAMSKARAS. Subtle impressions of past deeds.

SANYASA. Renunciation.

SANYASI. One who has taken the vows of renunciation.

SATSANGA. The company of a wise person.

SATTVA. One of the attributes of nature; the energy that tends to move upward and is light and bright; the force of illumination.

SATTVIC. Pertaining to uplifting thoughts, feelings, and energies; pure in quality and behavior.

SHAKTI. Power; force; energy.

SHAKTIPATA. The bestowing of spiritual energy; the descent of divine grace; transmission of spiritual wisdom.

SHAKTISM. The school of philosophy that advocates the supremacy of *shakti*. The philosophy that claims the whole world evolves from *shakti* and that even in its manifest form, exists in the realm of *shakti* and ultimately dissolves back into *shakti*.

SHAMA. Quietude of mind; tranquility; equanimity; composure.

SHASTRA KRIPA. See *kripa*.

SHIVA. The auspicious one; the transcendental being beyond all names and forms; one of the gods in the Hindu pantheon.

SHRAVANA. Listening to scriptures or teachers; the first step in the Vedantic method of *sadhana*.

SHROTRIYA BRAHMIN. One who is well-versed in the knowledge of the Vedas and lives up to the Vedic injunctions.

SHRIVIDYA. The highest among all spiritual sciences; the culmination of all the philosophical, metaphysical, and spiritual wisdom of the ancient sages. According to this system of thought, all that exists in the macrocosm exists in the microcosm. It is in this school of yoga one finds a profound discussion of *yantra*, *mantra*, *chakras*, and *kundalini shakti*.

SIDDHASANA. The accomplished pose; one of the traditional meditative *asanas*.

SIDDHI. A supernatural power which is achieved through yogic practices.

STHALA-SAMADHI. Casting off one's body while sitting in *siddhasana*.

SURYA VIJNANA. The mystical science of the sun; solar science; the science pertaining to exploring the source of the life force.

SVADHYAYA. Self-study; study of scriptures as well as study of one's self at every level.

SVARA VIJNANA. The science of breath; the science of *pranic* force.

TAMAS. one of the attributes of nature; the energy that tends to move downward and is associated with darkness and inertia.

TANTRA. A school of yoga which maps the spiritual journey in three stages: *kaula, misra,* and *samaya.* In the *kaula* stage, one learns a system of using all external objects as means for spiritual unfoldment. At the *misra* level, the external means are not yet abandoned, but focus shifts to practice of internal methods of meditation. At the *samaya* level, the practitioner is no longer involved in external, ritualistic practices but practices only the internal methods and learns the system of meditating at the *sahasrara,* the crown *chakra.*

TAPAS. Austerity; the method of yogic disciplines that help one balance the energies of the body—*vatta, pitta,* and *kapha*; enduring the pairs of opposites—pleasure and pain, hot and cold, and so forth.

TITIKSHA. Forbearance; tolerance; endurance.

TIVRA MUMUKSHA. A strong desire for liberation as opposed to mere curiosity.

UPANISHADS. A group of ancient scriptures, which are studied while sitting at the feet of the master. The great philosopher and yogi, Shankaracharya, wrote commentaries on eleven Upanishads, which are considered to be the principal ones.

UPARATI. Desisting from sensual pleasures; withdrawal of the senses so that one is not driven by temptations of the world; overcoming cravings for worldly pleasures.

VAIRAGYA. Non-attachment; remaining unaffected by the charms and temptations of the world; keeping the mind free from the worldly stains.

VASANAS. Subtle impressions of past deeds that influence the actions that we perform in the present; habit patterns; innate tendencies of mind; subtle personality traits.

VEDAS. The world's most ancient scriptures, which contain the wisdom of the ancient sages. According to Indian tradition, every single word of the Vedas is revealed. They are not works of human authors.

VEDANTA. The culmination of Vedic wisdom; the last phase of Vedic literature; the philosophy that expounds the theory of non-dualism.

VICHARA. Right thinking; contemplation; discerning thoughts; contemplative wisdom.

YAJNOPAVITA. The sacred, ceremonial thread that students of the Vedas receive when they begin their studies.

YANTRA. Geometrical diagram giving a visual understanding of invisible forces of nature; a geometrical figure laden with symbolic meanings, often used as an object of concentration.

The main building of the Institute headquarters, near Honesdale, Pennsylvania.

THE HIMALAYAN INSTITUTE

Founded in 1971 by Swami Rama, the Himalayan Institute has been dedicated to helping people grow physically, mentally, and spiritually by combining the best knowledge of both the East and the West.

Our international headquarters is located on a beautiful 400-acre campus in the rolling hills of the Pocono Mountains of northeastern Pennsylvania. The atmosphere here is one to foster growth, increased inner awareness, and calm. Our grounds provide a wonderfully peaceful and healthy setting for our seminars and extended programs. Students from around the world join us here to attend programs in such diverse areas as hatha yoga, meditation, stress reduction, Ayurveda, nutrition, Eastern philosophy, psychology, and other subjects. Whether the programs are for weekend meditation retreats, week-long seminars on spirituality, months-long residential programs, or holistic health services, the attempt here is to provide an environment of gentle inner progress. We invite you to join with us in the ongoing process of personal growth and development.

The Institute is a nonprofit organization. Your membership in the Institute helps to support its programs. Please call or write for information on becoming a member.

Institute Programs, Services, and Facilities

Institute programs share an emphasis on conscious holistic living and personal self-development, including:

> Special weekend or extended seminars to teach skills and techniques for increasing your ability to be healthy and enjoy life.

> Meditation retreats and advanced meditation and philosophical instruction.

> Vegetarian cooking and nutritional training.

> Hatha yoga and exercise workshops.

> Residential programs for self-development.

> Holistic health services and Ayurvedic Rejuvenation Programs through the Institute's Center for Health and Healing.

A *Quarterly Guide to Programs and Other Offerings* is free within the USA. To request a copy, or for further information, call 800-822-4547 or 570-253-5551, fax 570-253-9078, email bqinfo@himalayaninstitute.org, write the Himalayan Institute, RR 1 Box 400, Honesdale, PA 18431-9706 USA or visit our website at www.himalayaninstitute.org.

The main building of the hospital, outside Dehra Dun

Himalayan Institute Hospital and Medical City

A major aspect of the Institute's work around the world is its support of a comprehensive Medical City in the Garhwal region of the foothills of the Himalayas. A bold vision to bring medical services to 15 million mostly poor people who have little or no healthcare in northern India began modestly in 1989 with an outpatient program in Uttar Pradesh.

Today that vision has grown to include a fully operational, 500-bed, state-of-the-art hospital located between Dehra Dun and Rishikesh; a Medical College and nursing school, a combined therapy program that joins the best of modern, Western medicine and the time-tested wisdom of traditional methods of healthcare; a rural development program that has adopted more than 150 villages; and housing facilities for staff, students, and patients' relatives.

The project was conceived, designed, and led by Swami Rama, who was a native of this part of India. He always envisioned joining the best knowledge of the East and West. And that is what is occurring at this medical facility, 125 miles north of New Delhi.

Guided by the Himalayan Institute Hospital Trust, the umbrella body for the entire project, the hospital, medical city, and rural development program are considered models of healthcare for the whole of India and for medically under-served people worldwide.

Construction, expansion, and the fund-raising necessary to accomplish it all continues. The hospital is now one of the best-equipped hospitals in India, but more still needs to be done.

We welcome financial support to help with this and other projects. If you would like further information, please call our international headquarters in Honesdale, PA at 800-822-4547 or 717-253-5551, e-mail BMCinfo@himalayaninstitute.org, fax 717-253-9078, or write RR 1, Box 400, Honesdale, PA 18431-9706 USA.